Bedtime Stories
for Grown-ups

Bedtime Stories for Grown-ups

Fairy-Tale Psychology

D. Sue Gallehugh, Ph.D. and
Allen Gallehugh

Health Communications, Inc.
Deerfield Beach, Florida

Library of Congress Cataloging-in-Publication Data

Gallehugh, D. Sue, (date)
    Bedtime stories for grown-ups : fairy-tale psychology /
D. Sue Gallehugh and Allen Gallehugh.
      p. cm.
    ISBN 1-55874-361-8 (trade paper)
    1. Self-acceptance. 2. Self-esteem. 3. Self-actualization
(Psychology) I. Gallehugh, Allen, (date). II. Title.
BF575.S37G35 1995
158--dc20   95-32366
                                                                      CIP

Publisher: Health Communications, Inc.
          3201 S.W. 15th Street
          Deerfield Beach, Florida 33442-8190

Illustrations by Sheilah Anne Oscher; cover design by Jose Villavicencio.

*Dedicated in memory of
Dr. Clyde A. Gallehugh,
husband and father*

 ontents

 cknowledgments

We would like to thank our family and friends who offered to read the first draft of these stories, and waged war against some of the more painfully bad puns: Louis and Marcella Duncan, Nancy Dunckel, Lisa Gallehugh, Janie Hickerson, Jennifer Keller, Lisa Landolt, Larry Link, Joseph Lugo, Doug Manning, Mary Martin, Eric and Cindy Mills, Bruce Naylor, Joyce Naylor, Doug Smith, and Mark and Belinda Orland. Our special thanks go to Christine Belleris and Matthew Diener at HCI, for saving this book from the slush pile, and polishing up the rough edges.

ntroduction

Learning to love yourself is the foundation of all mental, spiritual, physical and social growth. This is not a narcissistic self-love, but rather an appreciation of the unique personality, talents, and perspective that we have all been given. People who love themselves are comfortable with their own beliefs, secure within, and willing to assume responsibility for their actions. Loving yourself involves examining negative traits and realizing that you can make positive choices about what you think, what you feel and how you act.

We have found that we can often learn more easily through an allegory, because it reduces our natural resistance to change and makes a more memorable impression. Laughter allows people to relax and let down their defenses so they can listen and understand. The storybook characters we loved as children are humorously used to illustrate the fundamental principles of self-love and growth. Combining our interests in humor and mental health, along with our honest critique of each other's writing, we hope that this collaboration between mother and son has broadened the perspective of our book.

Remember, take one step at a time toward your goal and surround yourself with positive, loving people who cheer you on!

People Who Love Themselves Try To:

1. Maintain internal peace
2. Say "no" when they need to and forgive when they need to
3. Express emotions without letting their emotions control them
4. Always have a purpose for living
5. Take small risks even when they seem scary
6. Give very little advice, but ask "What are you going to do about it?"

7. Practice healthy caretaking techniques that allow others to take responsibility
8. Make positive choices about what they think, feel and do by directing activities toward their strengths and away from their weaknesses
9. Stay flexible
10. Meet problems directly rather than avoid or go around them
11. Have long-range and short-range goals
12. Stay connected to mentally healthy people

People Who Don't Love Themselves:

1. "Drag their feet" so that other people will have to make decisions for them
2. Say "yes" just to please people when they really want to say "no"
3. Suppress anger or exhibit anger in inappropriate ways
4. Allow others to manipulate them with guilt
5. Do only those things that feel comfortable
6. Isolate themselves

7. Rely on external things such as good looks, occupation or social status to feel good about themselves
8. See no choice in what they think, feel and do
9. Want to place blame instead of saying, "Everybody makes mistakes. What can you learn from them?"
10. Think that life should always be fair
11. Are reactive and many times perceive themselves as victims
12. Take things personally

To demonstrate more clearly how to recognize these self-defeating behaviors and transform them into self-loving actions, we employed the literary device of allegory. So tonight before you go to sleep, get into your favorite "jammies," prop up your pillow and revisit your favorite childhood fairy tales through the eyes of an adult ready to learn the important concept of self-love.

Sweet dreams!

The Third Little Pig

ammond Deggs, the third member of the family of three little pigs, was a mason by trade who lived in the tiny hamlet of Boar's Cove. Naturally, he wanted to build a house for himself from bricks. When Hammond learned of the huffing- and puffing-induced vandalism of the home of his brother Oscar and Oscar's subsequent murder, he was terrified. He was so frozen with fear he couldn't go across town to warn his brother, Mayer. Instead, Hammond bricked up the beautiful bay windows at the front of his house, padlocked the door and cowered in the corner of his living room. The "pigs" at the police department (a term of endearment in Boar's Cove) called a short time later to report that Mayer also had been murdered and hamhocked in broad daylight. All the evidence indicated that the modus operandi was similar in both incidents.

As he hung up the phone, Hammond heard the voice he feared most. "Open this door, or I'll huff and puff and I'll blow your house down!" It was Big Bad Wolf, carrying out his threat to systematically annihilate the Deggs family. Hammond felt too afraid to confront the wolf, so he remained silent and waited. Over the next few weeks, Hammond added depth to his brick fortress. He thought that no one could hurt him if he could not be reached. Hammond's friends, the little piggy that went to market and the little piggy that ate roast beef, showed up to visit him. (They didn't invite the piggy that goes wee, wee, wee all the way home for obvious reasons.) Hammond could barely hear them through his new wall, and he squealed at them to go away and leave him alone. He thought, it's probably that clever wolf disguising his voice! Even the sweet pleadings of his fiancée, Frances Bacon, could not convince Hammond to come out. The most persistent piglets selling Girl Scout cookies were left with bruised pig's knuckles after knocking on Hammond's door in vain.

The voices grew dimmer as the wall grew thicker allowing Hammond to feel safe for a while. But as the months passed, Hammond grew increasingly lonely and felt more and more isolated from the community, and from himself. Once, Hammond had been very proud of his appearance and had used his Stairmaster until his chops were in prime grade-A condition. He had even used a curling iron to give his tail the perfect twist. Since the incident with the wolf, Hammond became depressed, and slowly he let himself go. He had considered the phrase "sloppy as a pigsty" laughable, but now it seemed all too true.

After many months, he awoke one morning and realized that his brick fortress had become a prison. He recognized that his fear of the wolf must be faced head-on, because the solitude and the worrying had become worse than confronting the wolf. Hammond lifted his sledgehammer and began to dismantle his prison brick by brick.

Outside, the town of Boar's Cove was thriving. Hammond's friends welcomed him back and told him that Big Bad Wolf died several months earlier from trichinosis, the result of undercooked pork.

They invited Hammond to join in their neighborhood crime watch, which had been helping to keep predators away, thus preventing their porcine neighbors from living in fear.

One evening, several weeks later, while Hammond was entertaining friends on his new porch overlooking the beautiful Bay of Pigs, they heard someone knocking on the door, followed by the distinctive huffing and puffing noise that they all recognized. Hammond and his friends armed themselves and headed to the door to meet their fear. When they opened the door, they encountered Big Bad's daughter, Virginia. Knowing she'd frightened them, she apologized for the huffing and puffing, and told them of her lifelong struggle with asthma. The pigs welcomed her to the group upon learning she was a strict vegetarian. After all, who's afraid of Virginia Wolf?

Remember:

to practice facing your fears is a
big step toward loving yourself!

Heaven
Helps Those
Who
Help Them

Elves

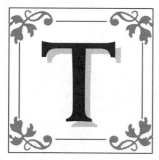here once was a poor cobbler who was not an effective time manager. He so often procrastinated in his work that he had to rush to get his shoe orders done on time. His haste often led to wingtips that didn't fly right, unscholarly oxfords and pumps that fell flat. With so many unsatisfied customers, the cobbler lost all of his repeat business and soon became as poor as a television repairman in Amish country.

One evening, the cobbler laid out shoe leather for the last pair of shoes he could afford to assemble, then settled into his recliner and scanned through the television channels aimlessly. His channel surfing soon lulled him into a deep sleep.

When he awoke the next morning, a new pair of tasseled loafers stood in place of the leather.

Before he had time to question the strange appearance, a customer entered his shop and bought the shoes on the spot. The cobbler was able to charge a substantial price because of the fine quality, enabling him to afford the material to make two new pairs of shoes. Again, he laid out the leather and then dozed off in front of his television.

The shoemaker awoke the next morning to find a beautiful hand-stitched pair of boots and an elegant pair of high heels. The first couple through the door paid for the shoes handsomely, and the cobbler immediately bought more shoe supplies.

The following night, the cobbler set out the materials and pretended to snore in his chair while he kept one eye open to watch his store. As his eyelids grew heavy, he suddenly saw a shimmering band of gold followed by the appearance of two tiny men with pointed ears. He knew they were elves because his mother had often spoken of them in his childhood bed-time stories. The cobbler sat awestruck as the elves produced tiny hammers and worked at a blinding speed until the leather was transformed into a wide array of finely-crafted footwear.

The cobbler could not control his excitement at this wonder, and he blurted out his appreciation to the industrious pixies. He told them that he was a failure as a cobbler and begged them to continue to help him. The elves felt obligated, because the cobbler was obviously needy, so they agreed.

News of the cobbler's wondrous new line of shoes spread quickly. The orders poured in, making the cobbler very wealthy and his new found elfin workers very tired. After many weeks passed, the cobbler felt himself growing bitter toward the elves, and he stopped complimenting their work. He felt more than a little jealous that his shoe work was never up to their standard of quality. He made casual "just joking" remarks about their height and their pointed ears, but there was always a tinge of anger in his sarcasm. He lost respect for the elves because they allowed themselves to be used by him.

Likewise, the elves had grown tired of their caretaking situation. The cobbler was draining their energy without so much as a "thank you." They feared confronting the cobbler, because they knew that he would manipulate the conversation to make them feel guilty.

On Saint Patrick's Day, the elves took a vacation to hang out with some of their leprechaun buddies. During their absence, one of the cobbler's wealthy regular customers entered the store and asked the cobbler to make him a tailor-made pair of alligator skin loafers. The man told the cobbler that money was no object as long as the shoes were made in that same day. The cobbler hesitated for a moment, then agreed to the offer. The man's request was quite a formidable task, because it required fresh alligator skin to make the best shoes. Fortunately, the cobbler lived near a swamp.

Although the cobbler spent the entire morning wrestling with a decidedly inhospitable alligator, he felt surprisingly energized after the ordeal. It had been a long time since he felt useful. He carried his "trophy" back to his workbench and slowly stripped the skin to make the man's loafers. He paid close attention to the double stitching and measured the eyelets carefully. The result was a pair of loafers that would not "sit around all day." The cobbler felt an overwhelming surge of confidence when his customer complimented his work.

When the elves returned, the cobbler told them of his success. He asked them to teach him their craft, and they patiently spent time going over the finer points of tongues and soles. They even shared the secrets of the exotic oils they used to tan the leather. He graciously rewarded them with a new cherry pastry he had perfected. The elves thought it was delicious, so, in an effort to repay their kindness the cobbler offered to teach them his baking secrets. When they asked what the pastry was called, the old man replied that he had named it cherry cobbler, after himself.

The shoemaker was obviously not very good at naming things and later lost a wonderful business opportunity after he invented the first pair of beach sandals, but tried to market the shoes under the name "Big Toe Separators." More importantly, the shoemaker found his purpose in life because of his new attention to detail and his newly applied elfin discipline to follow through on projects.

And as for the cobbler elves, they later used

the shoemaker's baking secrets to create a vast cookie production company which they ran out of the hollow tree in which they lived.

Remember:

**to practice having a good balance
between giving and taking
is important for your self-worth!**

Cinderella,
Inc.

he true story of Cinderella may surprise you because it does not involve a cast of animated birds and singing rats. Cinderella was raised by a stepmother who had two daughters, Winifred and Della, from a previous marriage. Contrary to the popular story, it would not be fair to call Jennifer, the second-string mother, wicked. Even though Jennifer tried her best to treat all the girls equally, Cinderella pushed her new family away, overwhelmed by feelings of resentment and abandonment. Still bitter with unresolved grief over the death of first her mother and eventually her father, Cinderella feared that if she loved anyone again, they would also leave her. While Winifred and Della, who admittedly were not that attractive although they had great personalities, used

to include Cinderella in their plans, they eventually stopped bothering to ask her to join them because she repeatedly turned them down.

Cinderella chose instead to isolate herself. She sat by the fireplace for hours while she dreamed of being rescued from her drab existence by a handsome young prince on a white horse. Once upon a time Cinderella was strikingly beautiful, but as the months passed, her luster faded as she wallowed in grief and unhappiness. She even stopped washing her hair and began to use food in an attempt to fill the void of her loneliness. Her loneliness did not get filled, but it did fill out her waistline. Even her well-tailored clothes became filthy rags as she lounged in the ashes by the fireplace.

Cinderella's stepsisters saved up their allowances to buy tickets to the annual Debutante Ball. They asked Cinderella if she planned to go to the ball, but Cinderella replied harshly that all of her dresses made her look fat, and that if her stepmother *really* loved her, she would buy her a ticket instead of making her pay her own way.

Cinderella believed that if she waited long enough and hoped hard enough *someone* would rescue her. As she stared up through the chimney, she wished on a star that something would happen to change her life. The answer came to her as a thundering pile of decayed leaves, soot and gravel dislodged from the chimney filter. Cinderella was knocked out cold.

When Cinderella awoke, Winifred and Della were standing at the sides of her bed holding cool washcloths to her head. Jennifer told Cinderella that she had been worried sick, because the accident had left the girl unconscious for several days. Cinderella could tell by Jennifer's watery eyes that she was telling the truth. Since her stepsisters had stayed by her side from the time of the accident, Cinderella's feelings of abandonment began to subside, and she was now able to see them in a new light. (Although, they were actually more attractive with Cinderella's blurred vision).

As she began to see more clearly, Cinderella realized that she had been playing the victim and that she had the power to make positive changes in her life. Several weeks remained until the ball, so she cleaned herself up and asked Winifred and Della to help her style her hair.

She lost weight by exercising and by drinking diet shakes recommended on television by a famous baseball manager, who claimed that they changed him from "pumpkin to coach." Soon she was even able to fit into one of her old, elegant evening gowns. In exchange for the money to buy a ticket to the ball, Cinderella offered to clean out the fireplace for her stepmother.

Finally the big night arrived. The palace glittered and the sounds of music and laughter filtered into the cool night air as Cinderella made her way to the entrance. The other ballgoers turned and stared at the beautiful Cinderella.

As Cinderella walked up the steps to the ballroom, she caught the heel of her shoe in a crack and it broke off. Normally, Cinderella would have scurried away in embarrassment, but the new self-assured Cinderella kicked both shoes into the bushes and entered the ballroom barefooted. Several of the village girls asked about her shoes, and Cinderella confidently replied that bare feet were all the rage in Europe. As the ball went on, several of the girls kicked off their shoes so as not to miss out on the new fad.

Across the room, Cinderella's eyes met those

of the prince. He was everything she thought she wanted in a man: handsome, with enough money to support her in luxury for the rest of her life. The prince moved across the ballroom and asked Cinderella to dance. When the prince looked down at her bare feet, Cinderella laughingly explained that she was wearing glass slippers that could not be seen.

As they danced, the prince talked on and on about his vast land holdings and told Cinderella that she must feel very lucky to be dancing with someone so handsome. He also managed to mangle each of her toes as he forced his way through a waltz. At the end of the dance, the prince told Cinderella that since she was the most beautiful girl in the kingdom, he would allow her to become his wife.

Cinderella realized that years of royal inbreeding had left the prince without much of a chin or a personality. Filled with her new sense of control over her life, she concocted a story about having to get home by midnight and then made a dash for the door. The prince conducted a valiant search throughout the kingdom for the girl with the "glass slippers," but everyone just thought that he was being a royal pain.

Relying on her own resources and talents, Cinderella soon started her own thriving chain of chimney sweep franchises using the slogan, "We Soot Your Needs!" And, of course, she lived happily ever after!

Remember:

to practice making positive choices about what you think, feel and do is necessary for self-confidence!

Little Red
in the
Hood

ittle Red was very fond of her grandmother, Marcella, and was never without the beautiful red velvet cape that her grandmother made for her. Little Red longed to visit her fun-loving grandmother, but she was terribly afraid to cross through the dense woods that led to Marcella's house.

The more Little Red thought about the woods, the more she built up a picture in her mind of the horrible creatures that could be lurking there. When she heard noises at night, she would envision flea-bitten werewolves, hobnobbing goblins and gourmet witches in search of a small child to add flavor to their stew.

One day, Little Red decided that her desire to see her grandmother outweighed her fear of the woods. She realized that she had been allowing her fear to take the joy out of her life, and she decided to face it head on. Little Red gathered up a basket of goodies for her grandmother, then headed for Grant Woods.

It was not long before Little Red heard a wolf whistle. At first, she felt complimented. Then she realized that there were probably not any construction workers this deep in the woods. Red pictured herself in her red cape as a do-it-yourself picnic lunch for the prowling wolf. Terrified, she turned to run as fast as she could in the other direction and fell into the arms of a handsome young man carrying an axe.

"Young woodsman, can you protect me from the wolf so I can take this basket of goodies to my grandma's house?" Little Red asked anxiously.

The man smiled sweetly, patted her on the head and answered, "The wolf can smell that basket of food, little missy. Why don't you let me guard it, and I'll drop it by your grandma's house when I'm through with my work."

Little Red quickly agreed and went scampering down the path with the assurance that someone was protecting her. When she got to her grand-mother's house, the door was already open. She spied a rather furry figure through the kitchen window and thought, "Even if Grandma had missed several electrolysis sessions, she would not look that hairy." It was the wolf.

It appeared to Little Red that the wolf was washing down the last of her grandmother with a glass of freshly squeezed orange juice. She was so filled with rage that she lost all sense of fear and charged through the door to confront the hirsute intruder.

At the same moment, outside the house, Red's grandmother jogged quickly up to the door and asked anxiously, "What's all the commotion, Reddy dear? You just turned my 10-minute mile into four minutes and thirty seconds."

"Oh, Gram! You're safe! I thought the wolf had eaten you," said the puzzled but relieved Little Red.

"Well, Marcella did say she wanted to have me for lunch," said the wolf jokingly. "Maybe I'm the one that should be worried."

The three of them laughed and talked for hours. Little Red learned the wolf and Marcella were old friends. Red said, "You know Gram, you've given me two really great gifts in my life.

The first was this fantastic hooded cape. Red goes with everything I own. But the second may be more valuable. You have taught me not to prejudge others based on appearances or my own personal stereotypes."

Just then, an announcement came over the radio: "We would like our listeners to be on the lookout for an escaped prisoner somewhere in the vicinity of Grant Woods. The Mad Axeman has been convicted of slicing, dicing and julienning in the first degree. He should be considered armed and dangerous."

Red remembered the handsome young woodsman who promised to protect her. She normally followed a "don't axe, don't tell" policy, but she felt more confident that day after her ordeal. "I'll call the police and tell them where to find that maniac," said Red. But as the words left her mouth, she spotted the axeman looming in the doorway. The axeman pulled out a knife and charged Little Red, but she quickly tore off her hooded cape and flung it over the intruder's head while she wrestled the dagger from his hand. Meanwhile, Little Red's Grandmother grabbed a handful of figurines from her cabinet and pummeled him with Hummels. The wolf tied up the disoriented convict with some of Marcella's industrial-strength yarn and then called the police. Professional matadors have spent years trying to master Red's "cloak and dagger" technique.

Remember:

to practice NOT prejudging others is a step toward liking yourself better!

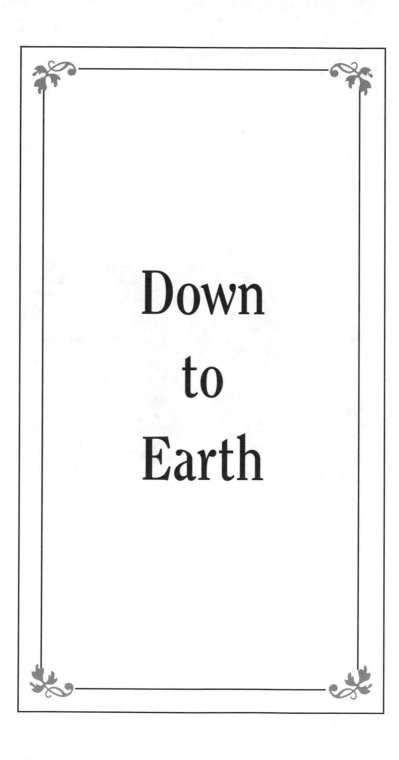

Down

to

Earth

ecause of her fair skin and delicate features, Snow White was treated by many with the same uneasy caution as an expensive porcelain doll. Her success in the "Miss Fairest of Them All Pageant" year after year only seemed to make matters worse. People assumed that her beauty had sapped away any glimmer of intellect. They also assumed that because of her looks and her status as a princess, she must be conceited.

Hence, Snow White was rather lonely. She felt unable to confide her sense of loneliness to her stepmother, the queen. Queen Jacqueline had heard that it was a stepmother's position to be wicked, so she did her best to live up to the image.

One bright summer day, as she was walking in the woods, Snow White stumbled upon a small cabin. Her curiosity got the best of her, so she peeked through the window and saw a table with seven little wooden chairs. Snow White could smell stew simmering on the stove, and she could not resist slipping in the cabin for a taste. As she reached for the ladle, she heard the sound of whistling and in marched seven diminutive men. The men looked at the princess and she at them. It was hard to say who was more surprised by whom.

"I'm Snow White," she said timidly.

"Yes you are dear," replied the leader of the group. "Perhaps you had better lie down until you get some color back in your cheeks. We wouldn't want you to fall face first into our Mulligan stew."

Snow White explained to them that she was actually called Snow White, and the gentlemen greeted her by rattling off their own adjective-laden nicknames.

"It must be hard to live up to names like that all the time," sympathized Snow White. "I spend a fortune on sunscreen to maintain my Snow White image, and I haven't been able to go to the beach in years. Actually, my real name is

Lisa. It's been so long since I've heard it that I almost forgot it myself!"

Snow White asked the tiny men to tell her their given names to prevent her from adopting any preconceived notions. She said that she was often pigeonholed by her name and appearance, and she did not want to make the mistake of prejudging them. The men seemed to breathe a collective sigh of relief, then announced their given names.

They told her how the townspeople had sent all the dwarfs to live together because their appearance disturbed them. Ethan said that although he had a degree in medicine, he could only get a job in the mines because the towns-people said, "that's what dwarfs do." Then he gritted his teeth and suppressed his anger, as usual.

" 'Dwarf' is such a horrible word," said Lisa. "It makes me think of those tacky, gnome-like lawn ornaments that share space with pink flamingos in the front yards of the aesthetically impaired."

"We prefer 'down-to-earth' instead of 'dwarf,' " they said in unison.

"Well, I don't think you need to use labels at all," said Lisa.

Doug, who had been standing in the back of the group, began to share his story with Lisa. "When I was growing up, I had a mild form of dyslexia that made it more difficult for me to read along with the class. The kids started calling me stupid and even called me the awful nickname that has stuck with me all these years. I actually began to feel like a dope, so I stopped trying."

One by one, the men revealed how they fell into the role that people expected them to play. Larry talked about how fear of his father's temper led everyone in his family to put on a permanent facade of happiness in order to not make his father angry. He said that he became so ingrained with people-pleasing that he often lost sight of his own true feelings and emotions.

Gary, who was labeled as having a negative attitude, talked about how his fear of rejection often led him to keep people at a distance. "People can't hurt me if they can't get close to me," grumbled Gary. Lisa and Gary discussed the importance of risking rejection in order to build trust and love, but Gary remained skeptical.

Lisa noticed that Donald kept nodding off

while standing in the corner. "Does he always do that?" Lisa asked.

"Yes. He's always so tired," Gary replied. "That's just his nature."

"I don't think that's anybody's nature," said Lisa. "I think Donald needs to make an appointment with a specialist to see if he is narcoleptic or suffers from Chronic Fatigue Syndrome. He may have something that could seriously endanger his health."

Donald awoke and groggily nodded in agreement with Lisa. The group talked more about challenging physical limitations instead of accepting everything as an insurmountable obstacle.

Greg, who had been sniffling through the entire conversation, announced that he was going to see an allergist first thing Monday morning because he was tired of playing a victim. He said that his sneezing attacks had brought him a little extra attention from the group, which made him feel reluctant to give them up. Lisa encouraged him to ask for attention from the group in positive ways, and Greg seemed reassured.

A man who had been sitting in the corner approached Lisa and stuck out his hand. "I'm Chase," he said. "I never talk to strangers because I'm basically shy, but I wanted to thank you for coming. You know, talking to you wasn't as hard as I thought it would be."

"That's the trick," said Lisa. "The fear of the unknown is almost always greater than the fear we feel when we are facing a challenge."

"Is there anything you are afraid of, Lisa?" asked Chase.

Lisa thought for a moment, then replied, "I guess I should be giving this advice to myself, because I've been scurrying away from my stepmother for years. I don't think that anyone really has a natural feeling of courage. The courageous people are those who learn to accomplish their goals and to stand up to their obstacles in spite of a feeling of fear. I think I'll sit down and have a talk with my stepmother when I get home. She may not be as imposing as I have imagined. After all, she very nicely offered me an apple for my lunch today."

Just then, there was a knock on the door of the tiny cabin. Lisa answered the door to find a handsome young man on a white horse.

"Good afternoon, Miss. I'm Prince Charming, and I think I've taken a wrong turn somewhere. Can you give me directions to Ed's Armor Emporium?"

"Charming," repeated Lisa. "What a lovely name."

"Well, it can really be a burden," said the prince. "I'm always expected to say or do something charming, and I'm always afraid that I'll use the wrong fork at dinner. Sometimes I'd like to just eat with my hands."

"Come on in," said Lisa. "Lunch is on the table, and we promise not to judge you if you want to put your elbows on the table or slurp your stew." The prince polished off several bowls of stew without the aid of utensils and ended his meal with a hardy burp.

"Charming," said Snow White wistfully.

Remember:

**to practice forgiving
yourself and others
allows self-contentment!**

Pea-
Brained

ne story that children's books never seem to get right is the tale of the princess and the pea. Prince Mark had been encouraged by his wise, globe-trotting grandfather to marry a real princess. Although he had searched through several countries, the prince could not find a real princess to share his wetland kingdom of Goose Downs. In his travels, Prince Mark had fallen in love with a beautiful girl named Christine, a poor daughter of a Texas toolmaker without a drop of royal blood.

As fate would have it, a real princess arrived on the doorstep of his castle during a terrible thunderstorm. The rain-soaked woman introduced herself as Princess Fahsod of Sardonica. The princess claimed to have fallen overboard from a passing cruise ship although she suspected that one of the crewmen may have nudged her after the snide comment she made about his bell-bottoms.

Because the soggy sovereign looked anything but regal, the queen devised a blue-blood test. She placed a single pea on the bed in the guest room, then covered the bed with 20 mattresses and 20 eider-down quilts. The chief export of Goose Downs was feathers, due to the abundance of water fowl, so there was always plenty of extra bedding. If Fahsod were a real princess, the queen believed, her sensitive royal posterior would not be able to stand even the smallest of lumps in the mattress. When the princess showed up for breakfast the next morning she said, "We are not amused. We did not get a moment of rest last night because of that uncomfortable bed. It felt like we were sleeping on concrete." (The princess' use of the royal "we" usually resulted in her receiving two entrees when she ordered at a restaurant.)

The queen proposed that only a real princess could be so slumber-sensitive. His fate sealed, Prince Mark reluctantly asked Princess Fahsod for her hand in marriage, even though his heart was with the fair Christine. Princess Fahsod readily accepted. She did not love the prince, but since her country's chief export was refrigerator magnets, her prospects for marriage were limited.

Despite a spectacular wedding with a guest list that rivaled the cast of Ben-Hur, the honeymoon was over before it began. The lumpy mattress was only the first of an endless line of complaints made by Princess Fahsod. She demanded piranhas instead of alligators in the moat, and she insisted that the boiling cauldrons in the tower use low-fat canola oil to discourage uninvited guests. When the prince was near, his bride painted on a smile, but when he was out of earshot, she ridiculed him and directed tirades against his helpless servants.

When the prince's grandfather returned from his travels overseas, he was a bit surprised by his grandson's choice of spouse. The retired king observed Princess Fahsod as she shrieked at the cook and sneered at the peasants. Because she did not recognize her royal in-law, the princess shouted at him to enter at the servants' door.

When the prince entered, the princess did an about-face and said pleasantly, "Hello, darling. I was just going to give this nice old man our new servant's orientation booklet and tell him a little about our castle."

"Uh, Fahsod, this is not a servant," cautioned Prince Mark.

"Indeed, no," the grandfather intoned, and introduced himself to the slightly shaken, but not stirred princess, who quickly departed. When the men were alone, the prince tried to explain his choice of a wife. "She's a real princess, Grandad," said Prince Mark. "I didn't want to disappoint you."

The grandfather asked softly, "Are you happy, Mark?"

"Well, married life has been a little rocky, but I know that a real princess will help maintain the royal order like you said."

"Like *I* said?" the old man asked, shocked. "I told you to marry a 'real' princess. That doesn't have anything to do with titles or money. I wanted you to find the kind of love that I found with your grandmother, a woman who was true to her ideals. She was real because she respected herself and others. My wife shared her feelings and emotions with me honestly, without filtering out what she thought I didn't want to hear. She may have been a scullery maid when I met her, but she was the most noble woman I have ever known."

The young prince realized that he had docked in shallow waters when he settled for Princess Fahsod, but, as future head of state, he felt compelled to honor their marriage vows. At first, the prince tried to change his wife's caustic personality through subtle hints, rewards, even pleading, but found that he was only exhausting his own patience. He sulked, realizing his situation was hopeless.

One day, while touring the royal pillow and mattress production plant, the princess' incessant griping to the prince about his choice of striped mattress covers started ticking him off. The prince stood firm and told the princess that vertical stripes had been a family tradition for generations. He wisely ignored her childish temper tantrum. While stomping on the overhead platform, the princess lost her footing. Even a biased judge would have given her a perfect score for the graceful swan dive she made into the vat of feathers below. The princess had grown fond of bathing in milk and honey, so when she emerged from the container she was resplendent in plumage. Upon discovering this, she ran into the street, squawking hysterically. Unfortunately for the princess, it was opening day of pheasant season.

After the kingdom's customary year of mourning, the widower prince returned to his travels. The prince felt drawn down south, and he knew it had nothing to do with his love of barbecued pork rinds. As fate would have it, Christine had just returned home as well. Her years in graduate school and a "Someday My Prince Will Come" complex had prevented her from settling down. When the prince asked Christine about her father's awl business, she explained that he had hit his third gusher this week. It turned out that Christine's beguiling drawl had hidden the fact that she was a Southern belle heiress, knee-deep in oil money.

Wedding bells brought joy back to Goose Downs, although the couple still needed to work on the happily ever after. It turned out that

Christine also had a fiery temper and was not afraid to let the feathers fly. The prince had learned from the ordeal with his first wife that even arguments can be constructive. They were each able to air their differences without bottling up their emotions inside. The new princess grew to love her marshy new homeland and developed a stronger love and respect for her prince, proving that sometimes oil and water can mix.

Remember:

**to practice sharing honest emotions
is an integral part of self-esteem!**

The Way
the Cookie
Crumbles

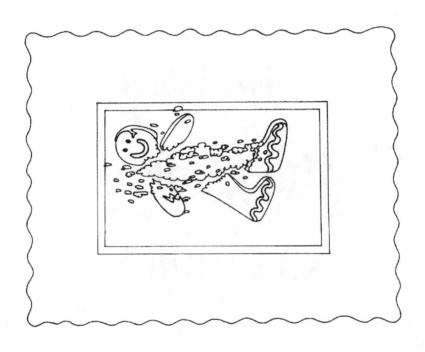

There once was a woman named Suzy who had grown tired of living alone. One day, she decided to bake herself a gingerbread man to keep her company. Suzy rolled out the dough and shaped the arms and legs, then used a cookie cutter to give him a perfectly round head. She gave her gingerbread man raisin eyes and used frosting to create a smiling mouth. She finished with a neatly frosted suit festooned with real chocolate chip buttons and a pair of licorice suspenders.

Several minutes after she had popped the gingerbread man into the oven, the woman heard a pounding sound in her kitchen. Alarmed, she flung open her oven door and, much to her surprise, out sprang the Gingerbread Man.

"Yeeeowww!" said the Gingerbread Man. "It

must be 350 degrees in there!"

The Gingerbread Man was seething with anger, but it was hard for him to convey it with the frosting smile baked into his face. Suzy scooped him up and held him closely, not knowing his true feelings. She gazed starry eyed at her confectionary creation and said, "Finally, I have someone to share my life with! And those chocolate buttons look so cute on you. I think I'll name you Chip." The Gingerbread Man was not able to communicate his anger due to his painted smile, so in frustration he freed himself from her embrace and jumped to the floor saying, "Try, try hard as you can. You can't catch me! I'm the Gingerbread Man!"

The Gingerbread Man ran out the door and into the street. His escape plan was rather half-baked because he did not have any particular direction in mind. As his tiny cookie legs grew tired, he stopped to rest by a farm. A cow from inside the fence called out to the Gingerbread Man, "I'll bet the grass on your side is sweeter than the grass over here." The Gingerbread Man was no grass connoisseur, but he did not want the cow to be disappointed in him so he sampled a bit of the local turf. Chip made a mental note never to order surf and turf in a restaurant.

"I'm Hownow," said the cow. The Gingerbread Man introduced himself and pretended to listen to the cow moan on and on about her long hours of cudchewing, and about the icy fingers of the farmer's son on milking day.

Chip was bored and ready to hit the road again, but he had to make due with his sugary facade. Hownow could tell that this cookie was a stiff, so she offered the Gingerbread Man a dunk in her milk pail to soften him up.

Several of Hownow's stomachs began growling as she continued talking to Chip. "Are those buttons real milk chocolate?" said the cow.

"I guess so," said Chip cautiously.

"Would you mind if I sampled a few? Farmer O'Leary's daughter is crazy about chocolate milk." Hownow then began a lengthy discourse on all the traveling salesmen the farmer's daughter had also been crazy about.

Chip was very fond of his buttons, but he did not want to disappoint his only friend so he popped them off his frosted vest and handed them over to Hownow. When the buttons were gone, the cow hurriedly said goodbye to Chip, claiming that she had forgotten to turn off the lantern in the barn.

The Gingerbread Man roamed the country until he finally found a place where there were others like him—Hollywood! Everyone in Hollywood was artificially sweetened, so they were not put off by his one-dimensional personality. He even made some new friends, Gingersnap Rogers and Fred Eclair, whose shallow lives revolved around dancing all night at L.A.'s trendy clubs. Gingersnap was somewhat of a creampuff and Fred was way past his shelf-life.

Chip did his best to please Fred and Gingersnap, but they often ridiculed him because he was made with unrefined sugar. Fred and Gingersnap also mocked his poor dancing skills, since Suzy, in her haste, had given him two left feet. Chip did everything in his power to keep his glamorous friends, but it ended up costing him an arm and a leg.

Tired of his hardening existence, the Gingerbread Man returned to Suzy's cottage, where he was welcomed with open arms. However, the Gingerbread Man began to get restless, and

grew increasingly stale as the weeks passed—
although his frosting smile never betrayed him.
Suzy decided to change the Gingerbread Man to
make him more into what she thought he should
be. Chip felt like he lost a little of his real self
every time he let someone else make his choices
for him. The Gingerbread Man did not want a
new set of almond eyebrows and a frosting perm
because he had grown accustomed to his face,
but he endured the changes silently because he
feared a confrontation with Suzy. Suzy did her
best to replace her cookie's chocolate chip buttons, but his hard exterior made it difficult. Chip
was also a little perturbed at Suzy for snacking
on his licorice suspenders in a weak moment, but
his smile continued to light up the room.

When Chip stood up after his cosmetic
surgery, his chocolate chip buttons popped off
and rolled down the table. He tried to retrieve
them, but with only one foot left, he lost his balance. What was left of the Gingerbread Man
landed in a crumbled pile on the floor, an inflex-
ible victim of his inability to communicate his
true emotions. Only his smile remained intact.

Suzy thought about baking another cookie

companion after her dessert deserted her, but realized that she would be unable to give him the ability to show the feelings that were essential for his emotional health. She knew that without this ingredient, anyone would fall to pieces—when the chips are down.

Remember:

to practice NOT stuffing your feelings increases your self-respect!

Unbearable

nce upon a time there was a family of three bears who lived in a modest cabin in the woods. There was a great big father bear named Bruin, his medium-sized wife, Ursa, and their young son, Theodore.

Bruin, an aspiring stockbroker with the Bear Market Investment Group, never had much time to spend with his family. Bruin had tried to cut his workload down to under 80 hours a week, but he feared confrontation with his boss, who was a real grizzly.

Ursa feared confrontation as well, and was even reluctant to discipline Theodore for fear that he would not like her. This lack of structure led to tantrums when Theodore did not get his own way. Theodore's uncontrollable temper once led to a rather messy and unfortunate incident when one of his cub scout friends dared to call him Teddy. Theodore often tested Ursa by telling her that he was "going to the maul," then would not return home for days.

One weekend morning, the bears decided to go for a walk while their morning porridge cooled. During the time they were gone, a girl named Goldie blazed a trail through the same woods. Goldie was given her nickname due to her golden hair, although it was rumored that the roots were brown. Realizing that she was both hungry and out of trail mix, Goldie spotted the Bears' cozy home and decided that she would invite herself over for breakfast. Goldie was more than a little self-absorbed and assumed that anyone would appreciate the pleasure of her company.

Goldie knocked on the door. When no one answered, she peered through the window. Inside, she saw three steaming bowls of high-fiber porridge. Goldie jiggled the door handle and let herself into the kitchen. She helped herself to a big spoonful of Papa Bear's porridge, but it was still too hot. Goldie was a bit of a perfectionist and often sent her food back in restaurants for this very reason. She tried Mama Bear's gruel, but it was too cold. Finally, she took a bite of Baby Bear's breakfast and it was just right, so she ate it all up. By this time, Papa Bear's porridge had cooled so she ate his as well.

Her hunger sated, Goldie wandered through the Bears' den and living room, looking at pictures and poking through their bear necessities. She had never developed a healthy set of boundaries for herself so she saw no reason why she should respect the privacy of others. Once, she had borrowed a favorite riding hood from her friend, Little Red, and returned it several months later with mustard stains.

Goldie even tried out the Bears' chairs. Bruin had a Bearcolounger, but it was really too big for Goldie's taste. Ursa had a rocking chair, but it creaked when Goldie tried it out, so she moved on to Theodore's bean-bag chair. She plopped herself down in it, ripping the seam wide open, and styrofoam pellets flew out of the broken chair, covering the carpet like a winter wonderland.

The lactic acid in the porridge was making Goldie a little groggy. She headed for the Bears' bedrooms and stretched out on Bruin's capacious and spacious king-sized bed, but the mattress felt too hard. Ursa's canopy bed had a cushy marshmallow mattress that didn't support her spine, but Theodore's waveless waterbed was "perfect," and Goldie fell fast asleep.

When the Bears returned, they were shocked to find the destruction that Goldie had left in her path.

"Someone has been eating my porridge," said Papa Bear.

"No one touched my porridge," said Mama Bear. "I'll bet it was too salty. I never can get that porridge exactly right," said Mama Bear apologetically, hoping to avoid a confrontation with Theodore, who always complained about her cooking.

Theodore growled, "Who ate my breakfast, and who took the secret decoder ring out of the cereal box?" In his usual dramatic fashion, he flung his bowl against the wall.

The Bears surveyed the damage in the living room with similar outrage.

"Someone broke the handle on my Bear-colounger," moaned Bruin.

"I'm sorry, dear," said Ursa apologetically. "I probably did that while dusting." (Ursa had an annoying tendency to apologize even when she was not at fault.)

"Who cares about your stupid chair," shrieked Theodore. "Look at this mess that used to be my bean bag!"

The Bears, sensing that the intruder was still in their house cautiously peered into their bedroom. They spotted Goldie sawing logs on the waterbed, and Bruin cleared his throat loudly to get her attention. Goldie awoke, startled by the Bears, but she did not apologize for her actions. Instead, while coiffing her peroxide-enhanced tresses and re-applying her ruby-red lipstick, she had the nerve to ask the bears if she could spend a few days with them while her apartment was being painted.

The Bears had never practiced taking good care of themselves by learning to say no, so they reluctantly agreed to let Goldie stay. Goldie's demanding behavior turned their lives into a nightmare. She had even talked them into buying her expensive home security package of "Goldie Locks and Deadbolts." They had not had such an unpleasant houseguest since Uncle Smokey turned his fire extinguisher on the candles on Theodore's birthday cake.

As the days turned into weeks, something unusual began to happen to the Bear family. Bruin grew so fed up with their narcissistic freeloader that he started saying no to Goldie's persistent requests for loans, insider information on stocks, and daily calls to 900-number astrology services. This assertiveness filled him with such a feeling of personal power that he was able to stand up to his boss at work and to negotiate a more reasonable work schedule.

Ursa spent the first few days sporting a "grin and bear it" attitude, trying to please Goldie by making everything perfect and apologizing profusely when Goldie complained. In time, Ursa began to realize that Goldie was taking advantage of her and stopped serving her uninvited guest breakfast in bed.

With his father more attentive to the needs of his family and Mom not allowing others to walk all over her, Theodore gained new respect for his parents. Theodore also learned something from Goldie's obnoxious behavior: He was able to see his own childish tantrums in a new light and he knew that he did not want to grow up to be like Goldie, mooching off well-meaning animals. He slowly started to take more responsibility for his actions. It also occurred to Theodore that if he did not apply himself in school that he could end up like his cousin Binky, riding a bike in the circus to support himself.

One day, Goldie whined that she was sick to death of porridge and demanded that the Bears have something different for breakfast. The next morning the Bears granted her request and served themselves up three big portions of— Goldie, lox and bagels.

Remember:

to practice setting personal boundaries enhances your self-confidence!

Wake Up
and
Smell the
Coffee

n the Land of Nod, it must seem like Princess Joyce had hit the snooze alarm a few thousand times because actually she had been napping for almost a century. The reason for her centenary siesta? Her parents, the king and queen, forgot their royal manners and neglected to invite a rather spiteful fairy to Joyce's first birthday party. The fairies who were invited had given her very thoughtful gifts like virtue, beauty, kindness, charm and a rather generous savings bond. Learning of her exclusion from this gala, the forgotten fairy crashed the party and, in her anger and humiliation, publicly put a curse on the young princess: "On her 15th birthday, after pricking her royal finger on a spinning wheel, Princess Joyce will die," shouted the irate fairy. The king and queen, naturally, were very upset by this display and promised to use RSVPs in the future. Their gesture, however, did not move the fairy at all. Just then, a rather fashionably late fairy, who had not yet given her gift (a stroller she had zapped up from a small pumpkin), offered to reduce the curse so that Joyce would instead sleep for 100 years after the finger-pricking incident. She also offered to put to sleep everyone else in the kingdom so the princess wouldn't be lonely.

The royal couple were heartbroken. They had always been protective of their daughter, but now they became obsessively vigilant. The king ordered that all the spinning wheels in the kingdom be burned and even banished the local quilters, cross-stitchers and knitters just to be on the safe side. Macrame could only be performed under close supervision.

Joyce was not allowed to play outside without the royal guards present, and her playmates were routinely frisked for contraband. These strengthened security measures led to a sudden decrease in her popularity at school. Also the princess loved animals, but her parents feared that a dog or cat might bite her and accidentally trigger the spell, so she had to settle for a goldfish. Her mother later realized that the goldfish bowl could possibly break into dangerous shards of glass, so Joyce's only pet, Sushi, was taken away and given a royal flush. She was not allowed to take horseback riding lessons for fear that she would be thrown. The princess offered to help the chef in the kitchen, but the staff was under strict orders to keep her away from the stove and the cutlery.

On her 15th birthday, Princess Joyce slipped away from her guards and searched the castle for her presents. Instead, in one of the abandoned towers, she found the disgruntled fairy disguised as an old woman with a spinning wheel. Anxious to try something new without the protective gaze of her guards, the princess sat down to spin some wool. But, alas, on her first try she pricked her finger and immediately went down for the count.

At that moment, the good fairy's counter-spell kicked in—everyone in the kingdom became drowsy and fell asleep in the middle of their daily routines. Luckily, Thad, the court jester, had finished his axe-juggling performance, so no one got the axe.

The weeds grew high over the next hundred years in the Land of Nod, and a giant, thick hedge blocked the entrance to the castle. Tales of the princess's beauty became legendary in the neighboring villages, and rumors spread far and wide that she could be won by waking her with a kiss. Several men journeyed to the castle in the hopes of breaking up the extended slumber party, but they could not penetrate the hedge.

On Joyce's 115th birthday, the spell was lifted and a groggy Land of Nod sprang to life. Yet another handsome suitor had arrived to challenge the hedge that day, but it parted in his path as he approached the castle. After hours of searching the drafty, old building, Sir Bruce of Addis finally found his sleeping beauty in the abandoned tower.

"Awake my princess," said the young knight. "The spell has been lifted."

Sir Bruce knelt to kiss his fair maiden, but after 100 years of sleep, her morning breath was enough to rust the visor shut on his suit of armor.

Princess Joyce opened her eyes and mumbled, "Just five more minutes. I was in the middle of a great dream."

Time passed and the princess grew to love her knight-in-shining-armor. (She even offered to polish it for him so that he would look good in his jousting tournaments.) They were married in a modest royal wedding ceremony, but they made sure that all the fairies were invited.

Because her social activities had been so restricted before the big sleep, Joyce had never developed any interests or hobbies of her own. Consequently, the princess lived for her husband. His interests became her interests and she threw herself into them fervently. Joyce groomed his horse, sharpened his lance and even made scouting reports on the local competition. She never missed a jousting tournament. Deep down, she was envious of Sir Bruce and his riding ability. Joyce longed for the freedom to ride into the countryside, but her sheltered youth left her in fear of the unknown. Her one attempt at breaking free, the spinning wheel incident, had unfortunate consequences not just for her, but for her entire kingdom.

The princess also masked her unfulfilled dreams by attempting to help others with their creative endeavors. She sponsored authors and poets with royal endowments, but she never committed her own story ideas to paper. She was a patron of the royal chamber orchestra, but when she tried music lessons, her awkward efforts embarrassed her, so she gave her piano to the chambermaid. All her involvement in the lives of others ensured that Joyce would not have time to feel her own emptiness.

Several years later, the princess ran into the spiteful fairy who had been shunned at her first birthday party. The fairy, who had just returned from an extended soul-searching sabbatical in Tibet, explained to the princess that she had learned the value in forgiveness and no longer held a grudge against the princess and her family for the invitation oversight. The fairy apologized to the princess for the little death-wish episode and said that she had let hurt feelings get the better of her. The fairy then asked about Joyce's life since her awakening and was given a detailed account of Sir Bruce's exploits. After listening for a while, the fairy realized that Joyce had not developed her own sense of identity.

The fairy offered to give the princess a magic amulet as a belated wedding gift since she had been out of the country. The fairy produced a silver cylinder and spoke in an eery, chanting voice, "With this charm, you will come to no harm." The fairy explained that the charm would allow the princess to develop her talents to their true potential. The fairy cautioned that the charm would not eliminate mistakes, or even failures, but that it would turn the mistakes into valuable lessons that would lead to future success.

The princess was delighted with the gift and felt a new found sense of freedom. She immediately went to her husband and asked him to teach her to ride. She fell a few times, but realized that each fall was helping her improve her riding style. Sir Bruce, who had grown a bit tired of his dependent wife, started to see his bride in a new light. Joyce was giving him more room to grow by stepping out of his shadow. Her return to music lessons was similarly successful. Joyce felt like she had finally awakened to life. Her first book, *How to Stay Lean at 115*, won critical acclaim.

Yes, the fairy did have to buy a new tube of lipstick to replace the "magic amulet" she had given the princess, but it seemed a small price to pay for happily ever-aftering.

Remember:

to practice developing
your own life purpose
allows you to discover
how special you are.

The
Naked
Truth

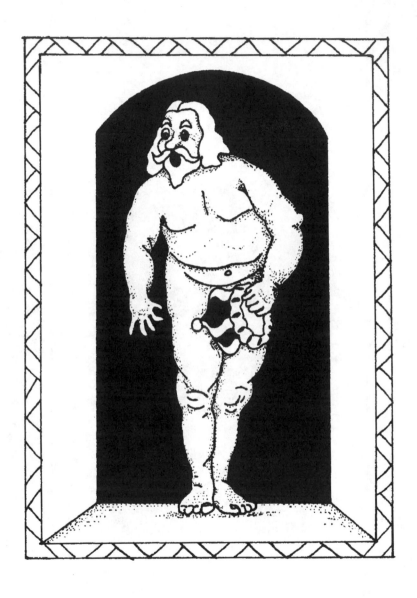

n the competitive business of eternal fame, Emperor Oloof of Hubris secured a solid place for himself in history. This was no easy task, given the notoriety other emperors had achieved. Some emperors had months named after them. Caesar even had a salad with tiny little fish in it, and that labor-saving way to give birth named in his honor. True to his flamboyant nature, Emperor Oloof penned his paragraph in the history books by making a bold fashion statement.

Emperor Oloof believed that clothes made the man. His rapid ascent up the royal ladder made him feel a little underqualified for the job description of emperor, and so he compensated with a warehouse full of the latest fashions. Nothing was too good for Oloof's closet. He hired actual polo players to model for the insignias on his sport shirts. Even his herring-bone tweed jacket was made with real herring bones.

When rumors spread that the finest tailors in the land were stopping in Hubris, the emperor summoned them to his court immediately. Emperor Oloof wanted a new suit, one that would stop and make people take notice of him, so he thought it fitting to see what these tailors could do for him. Despite the fact that it was mid-July, the lanky tailors were dressed in black turtlenecks and black leather pants. This com-mitment to trendiness was proof enough for the emperor, but they also had a business card to clinch the deal: Phligm & Phlamm: Finest Tailors in the Land.

The emperor tried to impress the men with a tour of his closet, but they sneered derisively and called his collection yesterday's news. Emperor Oloof proudly displayed his vast modern art col-lection, but they did not seem interested. The emperor was only interested in modern art him-self because he did not understand it but did not want the world to know. The tailors' indifference only made the emperor more intrigued about the mysterious men.

Phligm and Phlamm took the emperor aside and told him in hushed tones that since he was a special customer, they could let him in on a fashion secret. After they warned the emperor about not wearing white after Labor Day, Phligm reached into his bag and pulled out a big handful of nothing. The emperor was obviously perplexed, but the tailors explained that this was special fabric that was invisible to fools and those unworthy of office. They told the emperor that it was the perfect way to rid his court of incompetents. Since he could not see the fabric, the emperor was not fully convinced until they offered to cuff the pants at no extra charge. Phligm and Phlamm made a hasty retreat once the generous check was signed.

The emperor modeled the new suit at his next staff meeting. He told his advisors of its special properties, and they all seemed to pass the test. In the past, when the emperor asked his cabinet for honest, constructive criticism, those foolish enough to comply were left swinging in the breeze on the emperor's gallows. Actually, most

of the advisors had previously worked for his
brother Caligula, who made his horse a senator,
so the au natural outfit did not strike them as
that odd.

Since the next day was the emperor's birthday,
he decided to unveil his new suit to the public at
the parade in his honor. As the emperor marched
to the head of the parade, cheers turned to
stunned silence. Finally, a young girl whispered a
comment about the "royal scepter", and the
crowd could not contain itself any longer.
Everyone on the streets doubled over with
laughter. It slowly dawned on the emperor that
he had been duped. With his shoulders slumped
and his face a crimson that surpassed his throne,
the emperor marched back to his castle.
Unfortunately, the sales contract clearly stipulated
a "birthday suit" so no legal action could be
taken against the conning tailors.

After a few months of hiding out and serious
soul-searching, Emperor Oloof realized that his
empire did not crumble just because he showed
some vulnerability. With time, he was able to
laugh about his public overexposure. Some said
the joke about "having a ruler that is a few inches

short," came directly from the emperor himself. Oloof had grown tired of keeping up appearances for his subjects, and the invisible suit allowed him to drop the burden of a regal facade.

Remember:

**to practice being more accessible
to honest feedback is a big step toward
staying connected to healthy people!**

Eating
Me out of
House
and Home

ansel and Gretel lived with their father and stepmother in a small cottage in the forest. Hansel and Gretel's stepmother, Belinda, was the original wicked stepmother, perpetuating that ugly stereotype that has been the bane of stepfamilies everywhere. When Belinda met Hansel and Gretel's father, James, he was a very prominent, and financially successful, woodcutter in the village. It was the size of his wallet and not his strong woodcutter's physique that Belinda found attractive. James never really loved Belinda, but he agreed to marry her because he felt his children needed a mother-figure in their lives.

Though the family enjoyed a few years of prosperity, a sudden community-wide demand for aluminum siding and gas stoves, coupled with Belinda's access to the joint savings account, left James and his family nearly penniless. With the loss of the woodcutter's business, Belinda's clandestine plan to send the children to boarding school overseas was thwarted. But Belinda was a creative wicked stepmother, and she was soon taking Hansel and Gretel for long walks in the woods, followed by her version of hide and seek. Belinda told the children to close their eyes, count to 1000, and then try to find their way home. Belinda convinced the trusting woodcutter that she was helping the kids earn merit badges in survival skills. Since James was about as sharp as his rusting axe, he never questioned his spouse about her unorthodox style of parenting.

Despite Belinda's malicious intentions, Hansel and Gretel did learn to navigate in the woods by observing that moss only grows on the north side of trees and by using a small pocket compass that Hansel found in a box of cereal. One day, after Hansel and Gretel joined Belinda on another of her "nature walks," Belinda suggested a new game she had heard of called "pin the tail on the donkey." Knowing that his stepmother's "games" usually involved getting lost, Hansel reached into his pocket for his compass. He froze with terror when he discovered that his compass was missing. Still, Hansel was a resourceful sort, so he surreptitiously began dropping bread crumbs off the hoagie sandwich he brought for lunch. He knew that he and Gretel would be able to follow the crumbs back to their cottage.

Deep in the forest, Belinda blindfolded Hansel and Gretel and spun them in a circle to start the "pin the tail on the donkey" game. Belinda aimed the two children toward a tree. As they felt along the tree trunk searching for the picture of a donkey, the wicked stepmother wrapped a rope around them and tied them tightly to the tree. Hansel and Gretel had been to birthday parties before, and they quickly realized that Belinda was not playing according to Hoyle's Rules of Games.

By nightfall, Hansel and Gretel had managed to free themselves from their bonds. They set out to follow the bread crumb trail home by the light of the moon, but the crumbs were gone. Unfortunately, a group of wayward Lady Bluebird Junior Scouts and Survivalists had gathered the crumbs to make croutons for their annual Wiener Roast and Caesar Salad Sing-Along.

Tired and disoriented, Hansel and Gretel stumbled through the woods searching for a trail, but they only became more lost. When morning came, they could see in the distance the faint outline of a house on a hill. Hurrying as best they could, the children finally arrived, in a ravenous state, at the steps of a large ginger-bread-style Victorian house.

As they approached the door, they realized to their utter amazement that the house was made of real gingerbread. The door was solid chocolate with a marshmallow handle. Hansel could not resist sampling a piece of the gutter pipe, which was caramel-coated graham cracker. Gretel, who was a bit more impulsive, ate the entire licorice-woven welcome mat. Unbeknownst to the two children, they were being observed through the rock-candy pane windows. Without warning, a voice boomed out from inside the house, "Nibble nibble little mouse—who is snacking on my house!"

Before Hansel and Gretel could run away, the door burst open and they were face to face with a large elderly woman leaning on an enormous candy cane. "Trick or treat?" said Gretel in a weak attempt to cover.

"But it's November my child," said the woman with a knowing wink. "And unless you two are dressed as extras from Les Miserables, your costumes need a lot of work. Come in out of the cold. I would love to have you both for dinner.

"I'm Mrs. Bruja," continued the old woman. "I'm a retired algebra teacher, so I miss the smiling faces of young people."

"You have an incredible home," said Hansel, eyeing the cotton-candy curtains and the peanut-brittle tiled floor.

"Well, edible if not incredible," said Mrs. Bruja, "but I have an ant problem like you wouldn't believe!"

Mrs. Bruja served finger sandwiches, tater tots and bottles of soda pop to Hansel and Gretel, who hungrily devoured the meal. The children were having a wonderful time, but when Mrs. Bruja asked Hansel if he wanted to take a bath in one of her large stock pots, they began to get suspicious of the woman's real motives. Before they could act on their suspicion, however, they finished their sodas, grew very sleepy and collapsed on the floor.

Hansel awoke in a locked storage shed behind Mrs. Bruja's house. In the shed were a box of chocolate bars and two gallons of rocky road ice cream. He ate just enough to keep up his strength, thinking that a moment on the lips could mean a lifetime on the hips—of Mrs. Bruja.

Inside the house, Gretel awoke and was immediately put to work cleaning, cooking and fighting the house's ant, roach and mouse infestation. Though her situation seemed hopeless, Gretel remembered how her real mom had always encouraged her to take charge of her life. Gretel decided that she was not going to be a victim. She carefully developed a plan for her escape. Gretel noticed that Mrs. Bruja weighed herself several times a day. She surmised that Mrs. Bruja was obsessed with her weight, yet noted that the woman could not keep from snacking on the kitchen mouldings. Gretel also noticed that most of the latticework in the guest bathroom was missing and suspected that it had also fallen victim to her captor's appetite.

Years of loneliness had taken their toll on Mrs.

Bruja; she couldn't help but tell Gretel her life story over the following weeks. In this way, Gretel learned that the woman had a terrible self-image. Gretel also realized in the course of the talks that Mrs. Bruja was a witch. (The pointy black hat was also a big tip-off.) The witch told Gretel about her troubled childhood and how her parents never spent any time with her. Tears welled in Mrs. Bruja's eyes as she shared with Gretel her memories of no one being there to see her ride her first broom without training wings. The witch, obviously feeling sorry for herself, said that she was destined to live a bitter and solitary life because her parents had messed up so badly.

Gretel, unable to accept the witch's sob story, countered, "I'm not buying the soap opera story, Mrs. B. I haven't had a storybook childhood either, but I'm not going to let it ruin my life. You can't choose your parents or your childhood, but you can choose to determine your present and your future."

The witch was taken aback by Gretel's boldness. She talked with Gretel for several hours about how to make positive life choices. Gretel told the witch that bitterness was only hurting her and not those she was really angry with. The witch had been holding a grudge with Macbeth for over a century. Finally, the witch decided to check her emotional baggage without a claim ticket. Gretel gave the witch several lowfat recipes and showed her how to control her sweet tooth with more healthy dietary options. Gretel also convinced the witch that the fat content in small children would do terrible things to her cholesterol level. In exchange for Gretel's kindness, the witch released Hansel and Gretel from their captivity and gave Gretel a few handy recipes of her own.

With Mrs. Bruja's help, Hansel and Gretel packed up their belongings and some chocolate-chip shingles the witch gave them for their journey. Climbing aboard Mrs. Bruja's broom, they rose into the sky on an aerial tour of the countryside. The witch helped the children spot their family's cottage, then landed the broom in a clearing nearby. After a tearful goodbye, Hansel and Gretel headed home.

Hansel and Gretel's father saw them approaching the cottage and ran our to greet them with open arms. While the children were gone, he had not been able to sleep a wink and had spent many grief-filled nights whittling figurines. A local company had noticed the carvings and had offered to sell the hand-crafted items as lawn ornaments to the tourists. The figures started a craze, and the woodcutter had quickly regained his family fortune.

Belinda sulked at the children's return, but was happy to allow Gretel to resume her cooking chores. After Gretel prepared one of the witch's special recipes, Belinda mysteriously disappeared. The neighbors assumed she ran off with the milkman, but the woodcutter's new donkey would have a different "tale to pen."

Remember:

to practice facing problems directly strengthens your self-reliance!

Trollin'

on

a River

illy the Kid, the youngest goat of the Gruff family, felt a contempt for authority figures similar to the outlaw for whom he was named. One day, he decided to cross over the bridge to the Louis Pasture to seek out some tasty aluminum cans. The recycling craze had left his own field barren, so he assumed that there must be trashier pastures on the other side of the river.

Billy knew that there was a troll booth on the bridge, but he did not have any spare change with him to pay the toll. He had eaten his last quarter to tide himself over until lunch. He also failed to plan ahead, because he hadn't purchased one of the troll tag stickers that conveniently allowed his animal friends to zip across the bridge in the fast lane.

Out of options, Billy decided to try sneaking across the bridge without disturbing the emotionally maladjusted troll attendant. Surprisingly, the troll that guarded the bridge had not always been a vicious monster. He had once been a creative toymaker who brought great joy to the children of the village. He even created a line of ugly troll dolls. The dolls' hair was modeled after his own bushy, unkempt style. Unfortunately, the troll doll idea was stolen from him by a large toy company before he had a chance to profit from it. The dolls swept across the country, but the troll never saw a penny from their success. The troll had tried to sue the toy company, but years of failed litigation left him very bitter. He became so focused on revenge that he lost the creative joy and sense of accomplishment that he felt when he designed toys. The troll set up his troll booth on the bridge because he felt the world owed him something.

Billy the Kid crept across the bridge as silently as he could, but his telltale clopping alerted the vigilant troll beneath the bridge (which is probably why you never see any goat ninjas). Hearing the sound from above, the troll emerged from the sludge and silt of his riverfront home.

"Pay your toll to the troll," chanted the little attendant.

"I'm a little short on funds," Billy the Kid countered cautiously, staring at the troll's huge yellow teeth.

The troll barked, "You either pay the toll or I'm going to come up there and roast you with some mint jelly." Billy was so scared by the troll's threat that he coughed up his quarter from lunch and the barbed wire that he ate for breakfast, then ran across the bridge to safety.

Not long after that, Billy the Kid's sister, Billie, approached the bridge. She was named after jazz legend Billie Holliday, and tried to live up to her namesake in style. She often wore a black beret and dark glasses to go with her natural goatee. Billie's arrival was even more annoying to the troll, given her artistic preference for wearing clogs. Older and a little wiser than her kid brother, Billie knew not to take the rantings and ravings of a spiteful troll personally. Still, when given the "pay up or fry up" alternative, Billie relinquished her weekly allowance to the troll booth operator. "Wait 'til my brother gets here," Billie called back to the troll from the safety of the pasture.

Finally, Billy Jr. arrived. He was the oldest of the Gruff kids and had been named after his father, William. Billy Jr. felt some fear about confronting the troll, but he knew that true courage means facing fear. Billy Jr. held his head high and approached the bridge.

"Pay the toll to the troll, or I'll eat you on a roll," chided the spiteful attendant.

Billy Jr. had been around the meadow a few times so he was not drawn into the troll's "all or nothing" ultimatum.

"What's my third choice?" asked Billy Jr.

The question stumped the troll for a minute because most of the animals never considered that they might have other alternatives. "I don't know," said the troll. "What have you got to offer?"

Billy Jr. was proficient at creative solutions so he thought about it for a moment, and then remembered that the troll had once been a skilled toymaker.

"I'll tell you what," said Billy Jr., "if you let my

family and me have free and safe passage across your bridge, we'll collect a pound of scrap iron each week for you to use on your toy projects."

"I don't make toys anymore," said the troll sadly. "It's too much of a legal hassle."

"You just need a good patent attorney," said Billy, Jr. "My sheep friend at Shearem and Fleecem Legal Services can work through all the red tape for you."

The troll brightened a bit at his new possibilities. He immediately set to work on a new electric pogo stick. Each day as the three Billy goats passed the troll on the bridge, he seemed more and more at peace. His bitterness subsided as he decided to stop holding grudges. The troll had not realized how the grudges he held had burdened him, draining all the joy from his life.

When the troll's electric pogo stick hit the market, it became a huge success. With its success, however, fewer of the animals needed the troll bridge to cross the river because they could just hop across the water on their pogo sticks. Eventually, the troll dismantled his booth. He was once again able to make toys free for the village children since he earned a comfortable living from the royalties on his latest creation.

The three Billy goats Gruff were richly rewarded by the troll for their contribution. The two brothers were able to open the town's first upscale full-service salad bar, called "Tavern on the Grass." The goat cheese salad sprinkles were a big hit, but the villagers never acquired a taste for the aluminum croutons or the Bermuda grass garnish. Billie, who had always dreaded her job as a nanny, used her design talent to develop the successful "That Really Gets My Goat" line of angora and cashmere sweaters.

All of the goats learned a valuable lesson from the troll who had pulled himself out of the muck and mire of his embittered environment: "Grudge not lest ye be sludged."

Remember:

**to practice giving up bitterness
by NOT holding grudges is a big step toward
maintaining internal peace!**

The Low
Self-Esteem
Duckling

ollowing a rather long incubation period, Mother Duck stretched and carefully examined her new hatchlings. She swelled with pride as her adoring gaze fell on three daughters with perfect peepers and three sons with the rugged good looks of their father. Then Mother Duck spotted a large grayish egg nearby and assumed it had rolled out of her nest. She knew that even the best-laid eggs of geese and hens often go astray. Quickly, she sat on the egg, then settled down to lecture her new ducklings in the finer points of waddling. Luckily, all their feet pointed inward so there was no need for corrective shoes.

Three days later, the grade AAA egg hatched, and a large brownish ball of feathers emerged. Mother Duck named the timid creature

Samantha, but it seemed that everyone else referred to her as "the ugly one."

Samantha was shy and reserved, and she did everything possible not to draw attention to herself. She cringed when one of her brothers called her "Ugly Duckling" in front of the neighbors. Mother Duck tried to protect Samantha's feelings, but it was of little use since Samantha had already overheard her mother tell a friend that her daughter was more of an embarrassment to the family than the time Uncle Phil fell in love with a hunter's decoy.

When Samantha was a teenager, she had a hopeless crush on a popular mallard named Francis Drake, but he did not even know she was alive. This came as no surprise since Samantha did her very best to blend into the crowd. Samantha always drooped her head and shoulders to disguise her emerging neckline. Francis might have been the one duck that could understand Samantha's traumatic childhood, because he had faced vicious ridicule by other ducklings who made fun of his name. However, Francis learned not to take the remarks personally and even learned to laugh along with his friends about his name, which restored his personal power.

Sadly, Francis did not live through the next duck-hunting season. His friends saw the hunter and tried to warn Francis, but when a mallard yells, "Duck!," no one really pays attention.

A grieving Samantha decided to leave the pond and set out on her own. While heading away from home, she continued to hear the negative comments about her ugly appearance playing over and over in her head. On her journey, Samantha met a flock of geese. A very chic goose named Liv R. Paté told Samantha in a thick French accent that the flock was migrating to the Riviera for the winter and Samantha was welcome to join them. In response, Samantha droned on and on about how hideous she must appear and told the geese that she did not want their pity. The geese, who quickly tired of the whining Samantha, made a quick V-line out of there.

As winter approached, Samantha instinctively headed further south. On her way, she spotted the beautiful clear waters of Swan Lake and flew down for a better view. She was astonished to encounter the most beautiful, graceful birds she had ever seen in her life. Her curiosity outweighed her fear, so she paddled out to the seven swans a swimming. They giggled when Samantha launched into her well-rehearsed apology for her physical appearance.

When Samantha bowed her head and slumped her shoulders as she had grown accustomed to doing, the clear smooth waters of Swan Lake reflected her own image to her for the first time. She straightened her shoulders and held her head up high and gazed at her own elegant neck. Unfortunately, Samantha was battling years of negative comments from her family and a body image shaped by the image of the ideal duck, so she still saw only "the ugly duckling."

The swans persuaded Samantha to stay with them and, through a slow process of love and encouragement, they were able to show Samantha that not only was she a beautiful swan on the outside, she was also beautiful and loving on the inside. In time, Samantha's poor self-image began to change, and she gained self-confidence and self-esteem. She cultivated many new interests and learned to sing a pretty impressive rendition of "(Way Down Upon) The Swanee River." She volunteered her time with underprivileged teen swans and helped those who faced self-esteem problems in their awkward teen years similar to her own. Later, Samantha married and hatched a large family of cygnets, which she nurtured and loved. She had six daughters and one swan son—who incidentally invented the first frozen TV dinner.

Remember:

to practice changing your negative thoughts to positive truths promotes self-satisfaction!

The Lyin'
in
Winter

erald Grasshopper was a master of the fine art of hanging out and doing nothing. He usually slept in 'til around noon, then played a little fiddle before rounding up some food for lunch. Gerald always had time to hop by and mingle with his friends in the meadow and usually offered to mix up his favorite drink composed of rum, cream and creme de menthe to share with them.

One summer day, the grasshopper saw an ant who was carrying a piece of discarded french fry many times his own size. Gerald bounded over and stopped the ant to strike up a conversation.

"That's pretty impressive, little guy," said the grasshopper, who was stretching his long legs out in the grassy meadow. "You must work out."

"Can't stop to talk," grunted Antoinne the ant.

"Must store up food for the winter."

The grasshopper did not dwell on the ant's brusque behavior. He knew from past experience that the burden of holding grudges weighed him down too much to hop properly. With a mighty leap, Gerald continued on his search for summer fun.

As the end of fall approached, the dreaded robins packed up for Bermuda, bob-bob-bobbin' along, and Gerald breathed a heavy sigh of relief. Fortunately, the early bird had never caught him since Gerald always slept in late. Unfortunately, the departure of his predators also signaled the onset of winter. Gerald checked his food stocks and found that he only had half-empty jars of olives and cocktail onions. In previous years, Gerald had bunked during the winter with his friend J.C, the cricket. J.C. was not a bad sort, but he did tend to impose his own sense of ethics on the grasshopper. Earlier that year, however, J.C. had packed up his umbrella and headed out to Hollywood to seek his fortune in the cartoon industry.

The winds blew colder, and Gerald felt increasingly desperate as he knocked on the doors of his friends' homes. Most of them had already settled in for hibernation and could not hear his pleas. Truly, this was the winter of his discontent.

Suddenly, Gerald remembered the steady stream of delicious fast food leftovers the industrious ant had marched into his colony. Swallowing his pride, which wasn't filling at all, the grasshopper hopped over to the anthill.

The grasshopper called down the ant's hole and explained his desperate situation. Antoinne appeared at the entrance to his home and eyed Gerald suspiciously. Thinking quickly, Gerald concocted an elaborate story about how a praying mantis, who he naturally assumed to be religious, had stolen his entire stock of winter provisions. The ant was not fooled, but graciously offered the grasshopper food and shelter anyway. Even with Gerald's "fail-to-plan" diet, it was a struggle for Antoinne to pull him through the tiny opening.

The old adage, "there's no such thing as a free lunch" proved to be true: the grasshopper's fee was a seemingly endless lecture from the ant on the evils of sloth and the great rewards of hard work and perseverance. Even so, the tour of the ant colony impressed the grasshopper to no small extent. First, he was shown the War Room, where the army ants planned military strategy. Next, the carpenter ants proudly displayed their workshop, but Gerald made a quick exit when they began to sing an acapella version of "Close to You." He was even granted an audience with Her Royal Highness, the queen of the colony.

Surprisingly, when Antoinne tried to introduce the grasshopper to his own family, he stumbled on the names of his own three daughters, Beth, Lana and Sarah, getting the girls' names out of order. The ant's wife, Jean Louise rolled her eyes and returned silently to the kitchen.

Later, the ant explained to the grasshopper that it was because he loved his family that he was not able to spend much time with them. Antoinne believed that it was the duty of the family breadwinner to provide material support, and that his daughters would grow to understand his negligent behavior towards them.

Thinking about what the ant said and how unhappy his family seemed, the grasshopper gazed at the enormous mountain of food that Antoinne had collected. It could have easily fed the ant family for generations to come. Gerald knew the one thing he could give the ant and his family was a good time, so he invited the ant family to gather around while he rubbed his back legs together and produced a beautiful melodic sound. The children danced and sang, and everyone in the family had more fun than they could ever remember.

As the season passed, the grasshopper and the ant grew to know each other better, and both learned a few valuable lessons from the other. Gerald learned to set goals, to plan ahead, and that hard work can reap great rewards. He realized that it was his music that brought him true joy in life, so he practiced and practiced until he was accepted as first chair violin in the New York Field Harmonic.

Gerald's new friend, Antoinne, learned to appreciate his family more. He discovered that his family would rather spend time with him than have a bigger home and food stock with an absent father and husband. Antoinne started planning weekend picnics for his family. He taught his daughters how to spot a good picnic site and how to avoid pesky humans who bring their food in airtight containers. Antoinne learned to delegate some of his daily paperwork to the new Scouts in Training because he finally realized that his true joy was teaching. He had always loved the strategic intricacies of a well-planned scouting mission, but he hated the long hours of walking because of his bad back. You see, he was the one with high hopes—who had tried to move that rubber tree plant!

Remember:

**to practice keeping your priorities
straight gives you a sense
of well-being!**

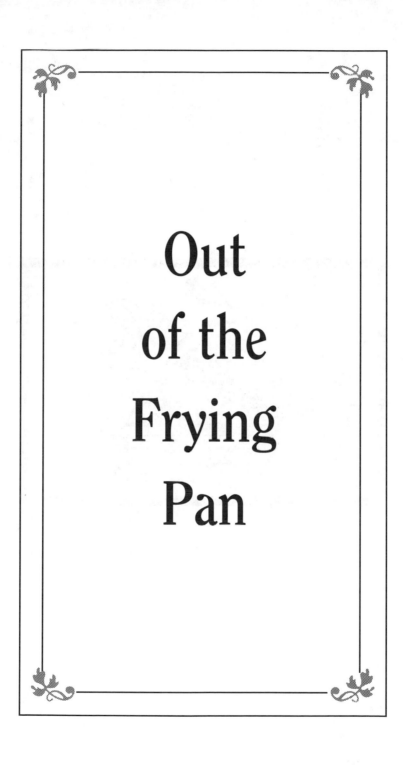

Out
of the
Frying
Pan

hicken Little sought shelter from the roasting sun under a spreading oak tree. Just as she fell asleep and began to dream about a peck on the cheek from Cordon Bleu, her fantasy French lover, she was struck on the head by a wayward acorn. Unlike Sir Isaac Newton, who, when a fig landed on his head, was inspired to develop the popular fig-filled cookies that bear his name today, Chicken Little, who was more than a little chicken, immediately panicked. She assumed the worst and ran off to warn her friends that the sky was falling.

First, she rushed to the home of Turkey Lurkey but, because it was near the end of November, Lurkey had barricaded himself behind his door. Chicken Little yelled in to him that the sky was falling, but Turkey Lurkey did not respond, fearing a surprise attack by the Butterball people. He was not about to end up stuffed with cornbread like his friend David. The image of a pop-up thermometer was almost more than Lurkey could bear.

Next, Chicken Little ran to the pond of Goosey Loosey. Goosey Loosey did not panic because she knew Chicken Little tended to over-react. Chicken Little went on and on about the end of the world, reminding Loosey about Skylab and all those golf balls the astronauts hit on the moon that could come crashing down at any time. Loosey finally interrupted Chicken Little long enough to explain that she could not possibly join in warning the countryside today, because she had a gaggle of friends coming over to make posters for her "Down with Down" cam-paign. Goosey Loosey had been organizing friends to convince the local pillow manufactur-ing plant to switch from goose down to synthetic stuffing.

Undaunted, Chicken Little crossed the road to get to the other side where Foxey Loxey lived. Foxey Loxey smirked when she heard Chicken Little cry, "The sky is falling! The sky is falling!" Loxey continually preyed on Chicken Little's irrational fears and had successfully sold her inflated insurance policies that covered fire, locusts, earthquakes, bad haircuts, continental drift and attack by rabid dingos. Loxey even convinced Chicken Little to buy an expensive life insurance policy for her children, saying, "After all, what comes first, a chicken or her eggs?"

Unfortunately, Chicken Little arrived at Foxey Loxey's around noon, and Loxey had not yet had his lunch. Foxey Loxey pulled out an iron skillet and set it on the stove. Chicken Little tried to continue her conversation about the earth's imminent demise, but she was transfixed by the skillet. Loxey bantered on about his special "Sky Is Falling" insurance policy in order to distract Chicken Little, but when Loxey slipped and said "drumstick" instead of "deductible," Chicken Little's feathers ruffled. It suddenly dawned on her that chicken was the special of the day.

Chicken Little had a flash of insight and realized that if she panicked and lost her head, she could literally lose her head. Chicken Little took a deep breath, doing her best to calm down, and examined her options. The exits were blocked and Chicken Little knew she could not overpower the fox. Her only chance was to outfox Loxey. Chicken Little considered coughing and faking a bad case of salmonella, but figured Loxey would not be fooled.

Instead, Chicken Little told the fox she had a wonderful recipe for homestyle country gravy. Foxey Loxey perked up while Chicken Little rattled off the ingredients. As Loxey stuck his head in the pantry to pull out a bag of flour, Chicken Little armed herself with the iron skillet. A gentle tap with the skillet left Loxey unconscious and allowed Chicken Little time to escape.

Chicken Little was strengthened by her brush with death and began to view her daily challenges as opportunities for creative solutions. She no longer jumped to conclusions, expecting the worst possible consequences. She also became more active in making positive changes in her life instead of waiting for life to happen to her. She joined Goosey Loosey's crusade, then started her own social lobbying group to "Free Range Chickens." Drafting legislation, she successfully outlawed chicken cooping without a trial by jury. Her autobiography, *Out of the Frying Pan*, became an inspiration to poultry everywhere.

Chicken Little faced some hardships later in life, but she handled them well because she knew it was not the end of the world.

Remember:

**to practice creative problem-solving
by staying flexible
ensures pride in yourself!**

Jack,
the
Beanstalker

ack lived with his mother in their small family cottage. Though his mother, Camille, was hard-working, Jack spent much of his time in a vegetative state on the couch watching old sit-coms. He only pretended to listen to his mother, who griped at him about harvesting their small corn crop. Jack's "I'll do it tomorrow" response lasted for weeks until the corn finally rotted on the stalks.

When the cable bill came and there was no money to pay it, Jack's attention was finally aroused. The only cash cow in the Benimble family was the last of the herd, a cow named Bossy who provided all their milk and butter. Realizing Bossy's monetary value (and that without cable he would have to watch network TV), Jack set out to sell the cow at the town market, giving no thought to his family's future dairy needs.

Along the road to the market, Jack met a shifty-looking character in a shiny green leisure suit. The man's name was Jojo Lugo, and he first tried to interest Jack in a distributorship for door-to-door pedicure services. When Jack explained his dismal financial position, Jojo stopped his hard sell. Jack explained to Jojo that much of his income went to impulse buys on the Home Shopping Channel (he even offered to show Jojo his newly purchased solar-powered flashlight). Jack also bragged that he expected to reap some huge financial benefits from a bridge in Brooklyn he purchased several years ago.

Sensing a sucker, Jojo was quick to offer Jack the "one-time only chance" to purchase some special "deoxyneochlorinated beans which have been exposed to gibberellic acid baths under syncopated gamma rays." Jojo offered a full family-sized bag of the "magic beans" at the deeply discounted price of a single cow. Jack was always looking for a get-rich-quick scheme, and this one seemed ideal since he already had a farm. Jack quickly signed over Bossy's title and registration and rushed home with his purchase.

Jack's mother was infuriated by his careless-
ness, but she secretly reveled in the fact that
Jack's bad deal offered her many weeks worth of
"I told you so's." Camille flung Jack's bag of beans
out the window for dramatic effect, then continued her well-rehearsed spiel on "look before you
leap" as Jack hit his mental mute button and
stared off into space.

The Benimbles' humble garden had always
grown noticeably large weeds, but even Jack was
shocked the next morning by a bean plant that
spiraled into the sky, through the very clouds.
Jack was normally very fearful of trying new
things, but it struck him that nothing would ever
change in his dreary life if he did not eventually
take a risk. Jack Benimble was still rather quick
and agile from his old tournament candlestick-
hopping days, so it did not take him long to
scale the towering beanstalk.

Reaching the top of the beanstalk, Jack peered
over the clouds and was astounded to see a large
castle in the distance. Again, he faced his fear
and tested the ground beneath him, and was
relieved that he did not fall through the thick
cloud base.

As Jack walked up to the monstrous doors of the castle, it was obvious that he could never reach the giant door knockers. Though Jack was a little slow on the uptake, he soon realized that the inhabitant of this castle probably shopped at the Really Big and Tall Menswear Store. As Jack turned to flee, the heavy door swung open and a Calico cat several times his own size strutted out. Jack quickly decided that he would rather be inside away from this gargantuan feline, so he rushed through the open door.

Inside, Jack gazed up at the towering resident of the castle, who walked across a football field-sized living room and settled into a goliathan easy chair. Rodney, the giant, pulled out a golden harp and started to scat in a booming voice, "Fee, Fi, Fo, Fum, I smell the blood of an Englishman." Surprisingly, the harp started singing backup. Rodney had an easel set up in the den with an unfinished watercolor of an actual-sized sailboat. It was obvious that the giant had a variety of hobbies other than the typical giant pastimes of pillaging small villages, trampling townspeople and grinding up small children to make bread. Jack watched as a goose of normal size waddled over to the giant. Rodney picked up the goose in the palm of his hand, smiling as she honked and laid a 24-karat gold egg. The giant gently patted the goose and praised her extravagant display.

Jack figured that since life had always dealt him a bad hand, he would make it a little more fair by stealing the giant's harp and golden-egg-laying goose. As Jack waited, Rodney fell asleep in his chair and a thunderous snoring ensued. Jack tried with all his might to move the golden harp, but it would not budge. Giving up on the harp, Jack grabbed the goose which let out a ter-rible honking noise that rivaled any 5:00 traffic jam. The giant stirred, then scooped up Jack before Jack could make his escape through the door.

Jack pleaded with the giant not to eat him and quickly spun his heartwarming tale of hardship on the farm. Rodney smiled and assured Jack that all "people of advanced stature" were not militant ogres bent on destruction. The giant forgave Jack for the burglary attempt and said, "Life and most people are too short to hold grudges."

Rodney even offered to help out Jack's farm by

setting up a meeting with the giant's jolly brother in the valley who had made it big in the frozen vegetable business. Jack was able to get a bird's-eye view of the operation, and he established his own successful frozen vegetable business, helping his neighbors keep their excess crops from going bad. Jack found when he applied himself and did today what he had always put off "until tomorrow" that he had more respect for himself.

Jack's mom ran out of things to complain about, then discovered that once she stopped her constant chatter about her problems many of her old friends who had been "too busy" to see her in the past started dropping by more regularly. Mrs. Benimble realized that her need to control Jack's life came from a feeling that her own life was out of control. Jack's progress toward independence helped her face her own controlling behavior patterns, and she felt a new surge of freedom for the first time in her life. In the end, the only bossy member of the Benimble household was their newly repurchased cow.

Remember:

goal-setting is a big step toward taking good care of yourself!

Hen-Pecked

ou may have heard the story of the Little Red Hen and the grain of wheat since the Little Red Hen tells it herself at parties all the time. If, however, you have been unable to attend the more respected poultry social functions, I offer the following brief overview.

One day the Little Red Hen decided that she would plant some wheat, so she asked her neighbors—the cat, the dog and the duck—if they would help her. The cat said that she would not be able to assist due to a hair ball she had caught in her throat. The dog claimed it was the same day as the annual Postman's Convention, and he did not want to miss out on a good chase. Even her dear friend, the duck, declined because she wanted to be around to see her granddaughter's first waddle. The Little Red Hen forced a smile and said to her neighbors, "That's okay. No problem," but secretly she was resentful.

When it was time to harvest the wheat, the Little Red Hen called on her friends again, and again they each had a more pressing engagement: a tangled ball of string, a tick bath and a duck-duck-goose tournament, respectively. Again, the Little Red Hen hid her anger and disappointment, but vowed not to return their phone calls in the future.

The Little Red Hen gave her friends one last chance when it was time to mill the wheat into grain and bake the bread, but they all declined to help her. She baked her award-winning bread by herself and left it to cool on her windowsill. The distinctive aroma of freshly-baked bread wafted through the town, and it was not long before the cat, the dog and the duck were standing on her doorstep for a surprise visit.

This time, the Little Red Hen exploded from the anger she had bottled up and yelled at her friends, "I can't believe you have the audacity to expect bread after abandoning me in my time of need!" Her friends were naturally taken aback.

They apologized to the Little Red Hen and told her that they had not understood how important their help was to her.

The Little Red Hen sobbed and admitted to her friends that her anger was really covering hurt feelings, because she felt as if she were being rejected. She agreed to be more honest about her feelings in the future.

The Little Red Hen was used to taking on responsibility and took pride in saying she never said "no." Unfortunately, this led to her being assigned to endless PTA committees, charity fund drives for families who were victimized by the Colonel's Bucket o' Wings special, Poultry Without Partners meetings and her duties as secretary of the local chapter of HENSA, for "bright hens at the top of the pecking order."

The Little Red Hen found she was spreading herself so thin that she never had time to spend on her love of baking or the trashy Harlot-hen Romances that she secretly enjoyed. Finally, after a particularly grueling day of babysitting her sister's eggs followed by her typical eight meetings, the Little Red Hen collapsed from exhaustion.

When the Little Red Hen awoke, she was in a hospital bed surrounded by her friends: the cat, the dog and the duck. The cat gave her a beautiful crystal mouse. The dog presented her with a bushel of her favorite fresh sweet corn. The duck brought champagne, although he caused a small skirmish with the hospital gift shop when they misunderstood his request to put the bottle of champagne on his bill. But the greatest gift that her friends shared with the Little Red Hen was the secret to saying "no." Over the next year they taught her how to take good care of herself by turning down invitations politely when her schedule seemed too hectic.

Finally, the Little Red Hen was able to relax and actually even crowed about her new-found peace. As you know, usually only roosters crow, so she dispelled the old adage that "whistling girls and crowing hens always come to some bad end!"

Remember:

**to practice saying "no"
when you need to facilitates
your journey toward self-respect!**

By Hook
or
by Crook

he want ad in the newspaper read, "Staff Position Available—Responsible for overseeing a large group." Jeff was hired immediately. On his first day of work, he was handed a staff and directed up a grassy hill to meet his flock. Jeff was not really cut out to be a shepherd because every time he tried to count his sheep he fell asleep. He also resented the nickname Mutton Jeff that the townspeople gave him.

Jeff's first panic attack came when his mom, dressed in her new fur stole, brought his lunch up the hill. Without his contacts, Jeff assumed it was a wild animal going for his mother's throat, so he cried out, "Wolf! Wolf!" from the top of the hill. Fortunately, the villagers thought that it was a barking dog so they did not pay any attention.

Later, smoke from the town's incinerator prompted him to start yelling, "Fire! Fire!" Unfortunately, the hill stood next to a shooting range. The range's unsuspecting groundskeeper, who was picking up shell casings at the time, had his posterior poised in a most vulnerable position. His resultant injury ensured that he'd forever be forced to sit on an inflatable plastic doughnut.

Jeff's tendency toward hysteria carried over to his work environment. When it began to sprinkle, Jeff ran out and bought miniature raincoats for his entire flock because he knew that 100 percent wool would shrink in the wash. When one of the little lambs ate ivy, Jeff had its stomach pumped in case it turned out to be poison.

Jeff routinely shouted down a long list of panic warnings to the villagers, including: "Earthquake!" "Killer Bees!" "The Dow Jones has crashed!" "Bell-bottoms are back in style!" But no one in the village paid any attention to Jeff because they knew of his tendency to overreact. They remembered Jeff rushing dramatically to the emergency room with only a paper cut. Many also passed on the story of how he

attempted the Heimlich maneuver on an unsuspecting restaurant patron who was merely
coughing.

While gazing into the starry sky one night,
Jeff was sure he spotted a UFO. He did not want
to take any chances, so he rushed down the hill
to alert the town, but no one paid any attention
to him since a blimp was clearly circling the
football stadium. Only Eric, a reporter at Rumor
Mills Monthly, showed any interest in the story.
It turned up later along with a doctored "alien"
picture of a Pekinese wrapped in aluminum foil.

While Jeff was in town, the wolf paid a call to
Jeff's flock and gobbled up a few wooly appetiz-
ers with the sheep dip he had brought along.
When Jeff returned to his post, he realized his
mistake. Helen, Jason and Jodie, three of his
favorites, were missing. Their crumpled yellow
raincoats spoke of foul play.

Jeff waited and waited for the villagers to
respond to his cries for help, but no one came.
His view from the hillside gave him a unique
perspective of the small village below. The
mountains he had perceived as a child were
merely molehills to him now. As he looked

down, he realized that he had been viewing his everyday challenges as insurmountable problems. Jeff came to see how this isolated him from Cybill and Sam, his shepherd friends. Even his family distanced themselves because of Jeff's daily "emergencies." Jeff's new perspective encouraged him to come up with creative solutions for his real problems, while letting the imaginary ones take care of themselves.

Finally free from the burden of imaginary crisis management, Jeff could concentrate on taking care of his flock. One day, Jeff realized that the "extra sheep" he counted was an intruder, but, for once, he did not panic. Instead, Jeff devised a plan to expose the imposter. When Jeff casually tossed a frisbee into the flock, the wolf could not resist leaping up and catching it in his mouth. His cover blown, the wolf rushed off into the woods before Jeff could introduce him to the business end of his shepherd's crook.

The moral here is clearly: Look Before You Leap (to conclusions)!

Remember:

**to practice viewing problems
as challenges can make molehills
out of mountains!**

Let Your Hair Down

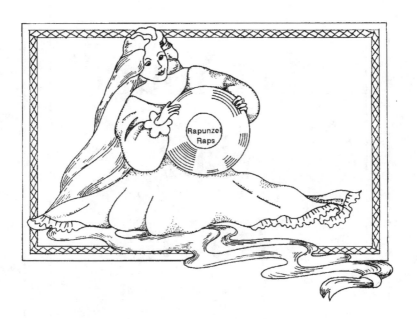

ost of us know Rapunzel as the girl who wore her hair long many years before hair extensions became fashionable, but there was more to her life than just shampoo, rinse, repeat. As a baby, Rapunzel had been locked in an ivory tower by a witch who won her in a poker game. Rapunzel was fairly satisfied with her drab existence in the tower because she had been isolated from the outside world. Margaret, the witch, told her horror stories of the crime and inhumanity in the world, and Rapunzel was glad that she was being protected from the dangers in life. Still, Rapunzel felt that there must be more to life than drying her hair.

Margaret had hired a rather inept architect named Frank Lloyd Wrong to design the tower, and he had neglected to include a door. This made it necessary for the witch to climb up to Rapunzel's room at the top of the tower. Since Margaret was too stingy to purchase a ladder, she told Rapunzel to drop her golden braid out the window so she could climb up. This was extremely painful for Rapunzel, but since the witch was her only contact with the outside world, she endured it.

Rapunzel loved to sing because of the great acoustics in the tower, but her voice was weak so she had learned to talk through the songs in a rhythmic cadence. One day, her whimsical song was overheard by the king's son, Tim, who was hunting in the woods. She sang, "I am Rapunzel / I live in a tower / brushing my hair out / hour after hour! / Sometimes I braid it / Sometimes I'd rather / Work myself right up into a lather!"

Prince Tim followed the sound of her voice until he reached the ivory tower in the woods. He was very surprised that he had not noticed the large white structure before. As the prince approached, he saw the witch and quickly hid behind a tree. Prince Tim had heard stories about the witch and did not want to end up like his friend Nancy who would spend the rest of her life in a terrarium after making a snide comment about Margaret's inability to accessorize.

"Rapunzel! Rapunzel! Drop the locks, kiddo!" yelled the witch. Immediately, Rapunzel lowered her braid and Margaret climbed up.

Prince Tim was intrigued and set out a plan to meet the mysterious girl. The next day, he arrived at the base of the tower and called out to Rapunzel in his best impersonation of the witch, "Rapunzel! Rapunzel! Don't be afraid to show me some braid!" Actually the imitation was very weak, though the prince could do a very impressive Jimmy Stewart.

Rapunzel threw down her braid and was very surprised when Tim appeared at her window. He offered to rescue Rapunzel, but she did not realize that she needed rescuing. As the prince talked to her about the exotic places he had visited and the interesting people he had met, Rapunzel realized what she had been missing. Rapunzel was reluctant to give up the safety of her tower, but Tim convinced her that she had to take some risks to experience the true joys in life. Luckily, the prince had brought along enough rope for them to make their escape.

Out in the real world, Rapunzel slowly built her confidence by taking risks and introducing herself to the townspeople. At first, some of the more jealous women shunned her because of her beauty. Rapunzel was deeply hurt by this rejection, but later understood that risking rejection is an integral part of growth.

Rapunzel realized that she had many new segments of her life to explore and nourish. First, she decided that she wanted to find her real parents. Prince Tim helped her locate them by having every woman in the kingdom line up to try on a glass slipper. (He had read about this trick in an article in *Better Homes and Castles* magazine.) Rapunzel had inherited her long, thick locks from her mother, so when a woman got her hair tangled up on the drawbridge, it became readily apparent who she was. Having neglected to equip the slipper with an Odor Eater, Prince Tim was especially pleased to call it a day.

Rapunzel's father, who had come along for the ride, cried when he explained how he had lost his beloved daughter when he tried to draw to an inside straight. At first Rapunzel felt betrayed by her parents for not fighting harder to keep her, but then she decided that forgiving them would help her to heal as well. Over the next few years, Rapunzel was able to rebuild trust with her parents and developed a loving relationship.

Rapunzel decided to continue to date Prince Tim for a while instead of getting married right away. She had heard of problems with storybook romances where the couple rides off on a white horse to be married soon after meeting. She also had to consider the fact that the prince's last name was LeDunckel and she was not sure if she wanted to introduce herself as Rapunzel LeDunckel for the rest of her life.

Tired of spending hours drying her hair in the sun, Rapunzel decided to invent a device that would free all women from this onerous chore. She had initial failures with the fire-breathing dragon model, but the lawsuits were soon settled and she returned to the drawing board. Rapunzel eventually patented an elaborate ox-driven blow dryer that used fireplace bellows and a cauldron of boiling oil she borrowed from the witch.

Margaret died several years later in a freak accident when her broom collided with a weather balloon. Rapunzel had made her peace with the witch and had even encouraged her to enter Sorcerers Anonymous. Rapunzel thought she could help Margaret lead a happier and more productive life by showing her the opportunities that were available to her. Rapunzel realized after months of coaxing, confronting and cajoling the witch that everyone has to make his or her own choices about change. In her will, the witch left Rapunzel the ivory tower and several dozen mason jars filled with lizard tails, eye-of-newt and something that looked like beef jerky. Rapunzel did not have any sentimental attachments to the tower, but she did not dismiss her time there. It had allowed her a chance for introspection that few are able to achieve in their lifetimes. Rapunzel sold the tower to an ivory poacher who had plans to whittle it down into scrimshaw, cameos and piano keys.

Rapunzel, now confident in her own identity and self-worth, decided to accept Prince Tim's long-standing marriage proposal. She used her Princess phone to call her friends Cinderella, Snow White and Sleeping Beauty to ask them to be bridesmaids. They were all active together in a variety of social causes, such as the Save the Prince of Whales Foundation and the Let Them Eat Cake Society which raised money to buy desserts for the underprivileged.

Prince Tim encouraged Rapunzel's unusual singing style and soon her music spread far beyond their kingdom. Her version of "I'm Going to Wash That Prince Right Out of My Hair" on Ivory Tower records went platinum. Of course, we all know her musical style as rap today.

Remember:

to practice taking small risks creates building blocks!

Your
Goose
Is Cooked

 ou may remember the golden goose from the Jack, the Beanstalker story. Actually, it wasn't really a golden goose. It was a goose that could lay solid gold eggs, but everyone still seemed to call it the golden goose. It's kind of like the Lone Ranger's horse. The Lone Ranger called him Silver, but even the most color-blind masked avenger could see that the horse was white.

No one is quite sure how the goose acquired this 24-karat skill, but it was rumored that young King Midas had inadvertently given the bird a "golden goose" when he plucked some tail feathers for his royal pillow. She was almost as impressive as the goose that lays eggs with pantyhose inside, but that's another story. The golden goose longed to lay normal eggs and raise a family, though her niece and nephew, Omeletta and Benedict, were a great comfort to her.

One day the giant had some friends over for a party. While the guests were trying to limbo under a goalpost, a rowdy band of burglars from Pennsylvania, known affectionately as the Pittsburgh Stealers, broke into the giant's home. It was not really a challenge since the giant's doggy door was the size of a two-car garage.

The thieves had cleverly disguised themselves to blend in at the giant's home. Sadly, Scott the Sot, who dressed as a beer bottle, had his head accidently twisted off by the giant's thirsty friend, Goliath. At this point, it was Giants 1, Stealers 0, and the thieves began to get nervous. Allen and Dale, although veteran burglars, were visibly shaken. They never should have chosen those salt and pepper costumes. When the robbers realized that even the giant's cuff links would be too heavy to carry away, they planned their retreat. As he headed for the door, Allen spotted a live goose in the living room. He figured that a goose this small would never be missed by the hulking guests who had just polished off a small herd of buffalo on toothpicks. The proverbial wild goose chase began, with Allen and Dale finally cornering the feather-ruffled honker in a broom closet. With the bird tucked safely under his arm, the salt shaker slipped stealthily out of the giant's house. Allen and Dale were unaware of the value of their squawking treasure but when Allen chipped a tooth on his Denver omelet, he discovered that his hardboiled egg was more than overdone; when he held it up to the light, it glistened like Wayne Newton's sportcoat. Allen and Dale realized that their goose was literally sitting on a gold mine.

Allen quickly calculated that if the bird laid one egg a week for a year, he and Dale could both retire from their life of crime and live comfortably off the proceeds. Allen told Dale about a mutual fund that would safely diversify their assets in a long-term investment, instead of putting all their eggs in one basket.

But, Dale—who had masterminded the poorly planned break-in—had a different plan. He wanted all the money now. First, Dale thought about how the money could bring joy to his wife and family. Then he realized that if his wife divorced him, she would be entitled to half his share of the eggs. So he made a mental note to divorce her first and let her keep the kids. Dale decided that the kids would only end up begging for handouts anyway, then selling their stories to one of those tabloids. He planned to have a lawyer draw up a prenuptial contract so he could keep his money if he decided to fall in love with a supermodel.

As Dale's temperature rose with gold fever, he looked across at his best friend, Allen, and decided that he could afford to buy several new best friends if he had Allen's share of the gold. Dale determined that Allen would fall victim to a "hunting accident."

As Dale schemed, Allen was planning ways to use his newfound windfall. He would finally have the opportunity to quit his dubious occupation and devote himself to music. Allen had always loved playing the guitar, but he did not have enough faith in himself to join a band. He decided to use a portion of his money to build a symphony hall for the town. After all, the people in the town had given him so much, although sometimes at gunpoint.

Suddenly, Dale pulled a cleaver out of the

butcher's block, grabbed the goose and told Allen that he was going to crack open the piggy bank. Allen tried to explain to Dale the benefits of postponing gratification for greater long-term rewards, but Dale would not listen.

When the dissected bird proved to be hollow, Allen grabbed a carving knife himself and turned on his impatient friend. The results were messy and involved assorted flying giblets and giz-zards, but in the end the well-bandaged friends reconciled. Dale realized that he had let greed warp his priorities and that his true treasure was waiting for him at home. Allen still had enough fingers left to practice his guitar so he decided to answer an ad in the paper from Robin and his band of Merry Men. In order to pay their med-ical bills, Allen and Dale sold their only golden egg to some guy named Fabergé.

Remember:

**to practice appreciating what
you already have reinforces your
inner well-being!**

Dam
It All

ou may have heard the story of the little Dutch boy, but most of the important information was lost in the translation, so I'll fill you in on the details. One night, Morey was out walking his hamster Andy in accordance with the strict leash laws in the Netherlands. Normally, Morey walked down by the lake where he sometimes could catch a glimpse of the crazy Spaniard trying to joust his neighbor's windmill. That night, however, the streets were nearly empty. As Morey walked past the city's dike, which held back the rising lake waters, his hamster stopped to drink from a big puddle. When Morey looked up at the dike, he realized that the wall had sprung a leak. Morey knew that the tremendous water pressure could flood the town so he searched for a way to stop

the water. Andy, his hamster, was too big for the small hole so Morey decided to plug it up with his finger.

Seeking help for his predicament, Morey yelled to his artist friend Vinnie Van Gogh, but sadly Vinnie had recently lost his ear in a misguided Valentine's Day gift idea for the woman who has everything. Then Morey waved his free hand to get the attention of old Mr. Rembrandt, but the alcoholic painter—who spent most of his Holland days sauced—cheerily waved back at the boy who had become a human cork.

As time went on, Morey began to think about what a hero he would be to the town. He had won some recognition back in his track-and-field days when his wooden shoes caught fire in a relay race, but this town-saving deal would be front-page news. As Morey mentally dusted off some mantle space for his key to the city, he heard some rumbling behind the wall. Apparently, Morey had underestimated the effects of the stress and pressure on the structure. His last-minute rescue attempt was not dealing with the real problem behind the wall.

Those who were fortunate enough to see it

said it was a thing of devastating beauty. Morey rode the crest of the wave as the dike gave way and floodwaters engulfed the city. Afterwards, he also tried to ride the wave of his new-found celebrity. He released a top 40 Dutch hit called, "Your Two Lips Deserve Tulips Like Mine," and later posed as the cover boy for a local paint company.

The stress and strain from the attention he was receiving started taking its toll. Morey was getting almost no sleep and his personality began to change. The once generous, self-sacrificing boy was being written up in the local gossip columns for making his dates pay for their own meals. The embarrassing stigma of Morey's "Dutch Treat" has stuck with the good-natured Hollanders for all these years. Also, the Dutch boy was frustrated because his waterlogged index finger never worked properly after the flood, causing him great embarrassment whenever he wanted to point to something or tried to type the letters m, n, h, j, y or u. After the disaster, the town installed a pressure valve to relieve water pressure before it grew to dangerous levels. People in the town who had once ignored such

danger signals learned to regulate the water sup-
ply before it rose out of control. Similarly,
Morey learned to regulate his stress and pressure
levels by taking time to exercise, socialize, spend
time alone and rest. He found that this allowed
him to handle any crisis that came his way.

Morey, older and wiser now, did receive some
long-lasting fame in his community. The town
voted to name the new pressure-released flood-
gate after Morey and Andy. They called it
Morey's Hamster Dam. Everyone agreed that
calling it a dam was appropriate, given the long
string of expletives that Morey shouted during
his unfortunate surfing experience. A statue near
Haarlem is inscribed in honor of Morey, "who
symbolizes the eternal struggle of Holland
against the sea." The newly irrigated city of
Hamsterdam, the "h" is silent in Dutch, thrived
and later became the capital of the Netherlands.

Remember:

**to practice finding outlets for
stress and pressure intensifies the good
feelings you have about yourself.**